Praise for

THE EXPERTISE ECONOMY

"Everyone agrees that learning provides a competitive edge in an outsourced, automated economy. But what's the essential next step? In *The Expertise Economy*, Kelly Palmer and David Blake make a persuasive case that companies play a huge role in shaping the future of learning. This excellent book offers practical and evidence-based insights that can help CEOs and other business leaders challenge the status quo."

—Daniel H. Pink, author, *WHEN* and *DRIVE*

"The opportunity to scale new learning curves at work is an intrinsic career value for an ever-increasing slice of the workforce, and an imperative for organizations who want to stay in the game, much less ahead of it. *The Expertise Economy* offers a framework for leaders to future-proof the skills of their people and organizations."

—Whitney Johnson, *Thinkers50* Leading Management Thinker, bestselling author *Build an A-Team* and *Disrupt Yourself*

"Disruption in any industry is a process, not a one-time event. With so much change on the horizon, Kelly and David highlight the imperative firms have to harness learning to stay in the game"

—Clayton Christensen, Kim B Clark Professor of Business Administration, Harvard Business School *New York Times* bestselling author, *The Innovators Dilemma*

"Brilliant, timely and significant, this book blows the lid off the learning theories of the past!"

—Sean Covey, President, FranklinCovey Education

"*The Expertise Economy* makes clear the importance of skills in the corporate world. For most companies, understanding what skills your employees have, what skills they need, and their agility in learning new skills, will bring a competitive edge in the future."

—Nancy Duarte, CEO Durarte Inc, bestselling author,
Resonate: Present Visual Stories That Transform Audiences

"In *The Expertise Economy*, Kelly Palmer and David Blake make a compelling case for why it's high time companies make learning a core part of their strategy—and show how best to do so. As the economy undergoes rapid transformation, we should heed their call."

—Michael Horn, Chief Strategy Officer, The Entangled Group,
Coauthor *Disrupting Class* and *Blended*

"Timely, clever, and useful insights on how learning enables individuals and organizations to flourish in a rapidly changing world. Anyone or any company seeking to learn how to learn will savor these insights and master these principles."

—Dave Ulrich, Rensis Likert Professor, Ross School of
Business, Partner RPL Group, bestselling author, and
Thinkers50 Hall of Fame: World-leading Business Thinker

"It's critical for companies to develop and build a high-quality, global workforce that can meet the challenges posed by the Fourth Industrial Revolution. *The Expertise Economy* is must-read for anyone who cares about the future of their workforce and organization."

—Nick van Dam PhD, McKinsey & Company Partner,
Chief Learning Officer, Professor, University of
Pennsylvania, Nyenrode, and IE University, Founder,
e-Learning for Kids Foundation

"Learning has always been one of the secret weapons of the world's highest performing companies. Kelly and David's book unlocks this secret and is filled with advice on how to make learning a competitive advantage for any company."

—Josh Bersin, Industry Analyst and Founder, Bersin by Deloitte.

"*The Expertise Economy* shows how companies can use learning and skills as key differentiators to stay ahead of the competition and ultimately help close the widening skills gap."

—Jaime Casap, Education Evangelist, Google

"*The Expertise Economy* is a unicorn among business books. It presents a human and business reason to address the skills gap in a holistic way with suggestions for how universities, companies and individuals can work together to prepare for the future workplace."

—Jeanne Meister, Partner Future Workplace and Coauthor,
The 2020 Workplace and The Future Workplace Experience

"Technological change is going to make the skills of the workforce all the more critical for corporate success. This insightful and persuasive book shows how technology itself can be used to identify, provide and measure the skills that individuals need to thrive. The technological revolution will transform corporate learning and this book suggests how. This is a smart book about creating a smart workforce."

—Andrew Scott, Professor of Economics,
London Business School, Coauthor, *The 100-Year Life*

"It's true globally, and especially here in India, that in these times of great change the agility to learn is the only secure footing. *The Expertise Economy* is the definitive guide to business leaders everywhere on applying the process of continuously unlearning and learning in order to lead in the global market." —AN Roa, Global Head, Cognizant Academy

"It always comes down to the question of survival. When we think about work, skills, careers of the future, and the onslaught of technology, we need to ask if we are really equipped to thrive in a world that does not yet exist. But what will it take? *The Expertise Economy* gives leaders the answer to future-proofing the skills of our people and organizations. The book makes for a coveted read!"

—Ester Martinez, CEO & Editor-in-Chief,
People Matters Media

"In *The Expertise Economy*, David Blake and Kelly Palmer brilliantly capture the rapidly emerging reality where learning is no longer episodic but 'pre-K to gray' and skilling is perpetual and expertise a critical and evolving workforce currency. CEOs not in sync with this thinking need to quickly adapt to this new reality and can learn a lot from this timely and insightful book."

—Deborah Quazzo, Managing Partner GSV Accelerate Fund,
Cofounder ASU GSV Summit

THE EXPERTISE ECONOMY

How the smartest companies use learning to engage, compete, and succeed

KELLY PALMER
and DAVID BLAKE

n*b*

NICHOLAS BREALEY
PUBLISHING

BOSTON • LONDON

First published in 2018 by Nicholas Brealey Publishing
An imprint of John Murray Press

An Hachette UK company

23 22 21 20 19 18   1 2 3 4 5 6 7 8 9 10

A CIP catalogue record for this title is available from the British Library

Library of Congress Cataloging-in-Publication Data
Names: Palmer, Kelly– author. | Blake, David– author.
Title: The expertise economy : how the smartest companies use learning to engage,
compete, and succeed / Kelly Palmer and David Blake.
Description: Boston, MA : Nicholas Brealey Publishing, 2018. | Includes index.
Identifiers: LCCN 2018016520 (print) | LCCN 2018019788 (ebook) |
ISBN 9781473677012 (ebook) | ISBN 9781473677036 (library ebook) |
ISBN 9781473677005 (hardcover)
Subjects: LCSH: Employees—Training of. | Expertise. | Organizational learning.
Classification: LCC HF5549.5.T7 (ebook) | LCC HF5549.5.T7 P265 2018 (print) |
DDC 658.3/124—dc23
LC record available at https://lccn.loc.gov/2018016520

ISBN 978-1-47367-700-5
US eBook 978-1-47367-701-2
UK eBook 978-1-47367-702-9

Printed and bound in the United States of America.

John Murray Press policy is to use papers that are natural, renewable and
recyclable products and made from wood grown in sustainable forests.
The logging and manufacturing processes are expected to conform to the
environmental regulations of the country of origin.

John Murray Press Ltd
Carmelite House
50 Victoria Embankment
London EC4Y 0DZ
Tel: 020 3122 6000

Nicholas Brealey Publishing
Hachette Book Group
53 State Street
Boston, MA 02109, USA
Tel: (617) 263 1834

www.nbuspublishing.com

For my son, Cameron, who inspires me every day.
And for my mom, who inspires me still.

Kelly Palmer
San Francisco, 2018

TABLE OF CONTENTS

Acknowledgements   xi
About the Authors   xiii

Introduction   xv

Chapter 1: How We Really Learn   1

Chapter 2: Make Learning a Competitive Advantage   23

Chapter 3: Embrace Personalized Learning   45

Chapter 4: Combat Content Overload   61

Chapter 5: Understand the Power of Peers   83

Chapter 6: Succeed with the Right Technology   107

Chapter 7: Analyze Skills with Data and Insights   131

Chapter 8: Make Expertise Count   147

Conclusion: The Future Is Already Here   171

Endnotes   191
Index   207

ACKNOWLEDGEMENTS

Writing a book involves so many more people than you might think, and we want to thank those who helped us along the way.

A big thank you to all the people who took time out of their busy schedules to be interviewed for the book: Bror Saxberg, Jaime Casup, Joanne Heyman, Rico Rodriguez, Tim Munden, Janice Burns, Tim Quinlan, Susie Lee, Wouter De Bres, Mikel Blake, Andrew Scott, Nigel Paine, Karie Willyerd, Alan Walton, Maksim Ovsyannikov, Tony Gagliardo, James Densmore, William Arruda, and Dale Stephens.

The Edtech world would not be the same without these forward thinking pioneers: Emily Foote, Aaron Hurst, Sam Herring, and Anne Fulton— thanks for letting us tell your stories.

Thanks to Sal Khan, Todd Rose, Whitney Johnson, and Clayton Christensen for their time and thought leadership and for giving us such great insights into the future of work and learning.

Our gratitude to Christopher Michel for the amazing photos; it was an honor to have you be part of this project.

Thanks to Chris McCarthy for his support and enthusiasm, and to some of our collegues who helped review drafts along the way; specifically, Sarah Danzl and Todd Tauber. And thanks to David Johnson and his brand team for their support and cover design.

Special thanks to Jonathan Munk who helped shape the narrative around skill credentials and making expertise count.

Thanks to Lisa DiMona and Genoveva Llosa for helping us get started with the journey, to Alison Hankey and her team at Nicholas

Brealey for keeping us excited and on track, and to Emma Murray for her partnership along the way.

And finally, thanks to Karie Willyerd for taking a chance and launching me into the world of learning. I'll be forever grateful for the opportunity, the mentoring, and the friendship that developed along the way.

ABOUT THE AUTHORS

KELLY PALMER is on a mission to change the way the world learns. A well-known thought leader on learning, business, and career development, she is currently on the executive team of Degreed and was formerly the chief learning officer of LinkedIn. Prior to LinkedIn, Kelly was vice president of learning at Yahoo! and held executive positions in learning, M&A, and product development at Sun Microsystems. She speaks regularly at companies and business conferences around the world, has been featured in Big Think, *Forbes*, and *Chief Learning Officer* (CLO) magazine. Kelly has a bachelor of arts in English/communications and a master of science in adult learning and education technology. She lives in San Francisco, California.

DAVID BLAKE believes that learning is too important to stay the way it is and has spent his career innovating in higher education and lifelong learning. David is the Cofounder and Executive Chairman of Degreed. Prior to Degreed, he consulted on the launch of a competency-based university and was a founding-team member at university-admissions startup Zinch (acquired by Chegg NASDQ: CHGG). David was chosen as one of the top 25 EdTech Entrepreneurs for a lab created by Teach For America and NewSchools Venture Fund and hosted at the Stanford d.School. He is a sought-after expert on the topic of the future of learning and work, speaking at both companies such as Google, Deloitte, and Salesforce and at conferences globally.

INTRODUCTION

In 2010, Sun Microsystems was delisted from the Nasdaq stock exchange after 28 years. Just 10 years earlier, they were a titan of the computer industry and at the top of their game, going head-to-head with then computer giants Hewlett-Packard, IBM, and Microsoft. Sun made computers and software that powered many businesses, including the New York Stock Exchange (NYSE), some of the largest financial institutions, and most of the major airlines. They also created Java, an innovative programming language that is still being used by the majority of software developers worldwide. The crash of 2001 devastated hundreds of internet and computer companies, but neither the analysts nor Sun's close to 40,000 employees could have predicted Sun would completely collapse or that its stock price would plummet and lose 75 percent of its value in just one year. In the end, Oracle agreed to buy Sun for $7.4 billion.[1] Just two years earlier, Sun had been valued at $65 billion.

Facebook took over Sun's Silicon Valley campus and kept the Sun logo on the back of its signage as a reminder of what can happen to a successful company if you don't adapt quickly.[2] But Sun is only one of many companies to suffer obsolescence, and company disruption is only going to be compounded in the years to come. According to Innosight's 2018 Corporate Longevity Forecast,[3] at the current churn rate, about half of S&P 500 companies will be replaced over the next 10 years. Companies that don't reinvent themselves, don't think about digital disruption, and don't think about retraining and upskilling their workforce will be part of that churn.

The world of work is going through a large-scale transition—much like the transition we went through from the agricultural economy to the

Industrial Revolution. We are now in the age of digitization, automation, and acceleration—an age where critical skills and expertise will be an imperative for us to succeed in the economy.

A 2018 McKinsey Global Institute report states, "The task confronting every economy, particularly advanced economies, will likely be to retrain and redeploy tens of millions of midcareer, middle-age workers."[4]

Because historically we've only experienced these kinds of workforce transitions over decades, if not centuries, we are in unchartered territory, especially in terms of how quickly things are changing: "There are few precedents in which societies have successfully retrained such large numbers of people."[5]

The Workforce Is Not Prepared

McKinsey's study makes it abundantly clear that the workforce is not prepared for the disruption that's upon us: "Sixty-two percent of executives believe they will need to retrain or replace more than a quarter of their workforce between now and 2023 due to advancing automation and digitization."[6] If CEOs and business leaders are relying on a "hire only" strategy to get talent with the skills they need for their future, they will have to think again. Even the best universities are increasingly failing to prepare students with the skills they need to meet companies' hiring requirements.

Research also shows that both companies and graduating students are feeling the pain: 82 percent of employers say it's difficult to fill positions, while 83 percent of students have no job lined up after graduation, and 62 percent of students report that the job search is "frustrating" or "very frustrating."[7] Even more troubling, leaders sometimes find after hiring new grads that they are wholly unprepared to succeed at their jobs or to navigate the *real* world of work, especially in this challenging and rapidly changing environment. These are people with marketing degrees who struggle to create a marketing plan and cannot use the latest social media tools to get their work done, or MBAs who cannot read a financial statement. And, employers consistently see graduates from all areas of study who can't communicate well, either in person or through writing.

College grads are not the only ones missing critical skills. People who have been in the workforce for decades often lack certain skills required for success in their jobs. Today, the vital skill set for success includes learning agility (the ability to learn new things quickly), collaboration and teamwork, perseverance, curiosity, and the ability to question the world around you. If you aren't ready and willing to learn every day and keep up with a rapidly changing world, you can't and won't stay competitive. Gone are the days when you could graduate with a four-year degree and feel secure that you had learned everything you needed to know to stay relevant for your entire career.

Business Leaders Closing the Skills Gap

While government can be a powerful force when it comes to launching skills initiatives, it's companies and their leaders who need to lead the way. CEOs, like Randall Stephenson of AT&T, are doing more than just asking, "Do we have the skills we need to win in our business?" Instead their focus is on ensuring their employees develop ongoing skills through continuous learning. As Stephenson said to the *New York Times*, "There is a need to retool yourself, and you should not expect to stop." He added that people who dedicate less than an ideal 5-10 hours a week to learning "will obsolete themselves with the technology."[8] This includes articles and books, podcasts, videos, etc. People are learning a lot more than they think but don't always categorize it as learning, and we discuss this later in the book.

To these companies, it's becoming ever clearer that employees with the right skills can be instrumental in helping their company succeed. But the problem is that many business leaders are not asking the right questions. How many CEOs know if they have the right skills for their company? How many managers and leaders actually know what skills the people on their teams have? And how many employees have a clear view of the skills they have and what skills they will need for the future? The figure below illustrates the types of questions today's leaders should be asking.

Questions Leaders Should Be Asking

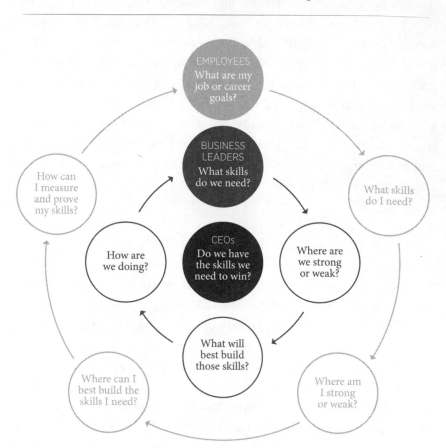

The Power of Building Skills for the Future

The most forward-thinking companies are being proactive in adapting to the shift in the workforce. During other major workforce transitions, we've had some time to adapt to the changes, but that's compressed today. Some companies are still pondering how work is changing, but digital disruption has been advancing for several decades now and it's no longer something of the future—it's happening right now.

Expertise has never been so crucial to a person's or company's success as it is today. Companies like Unilever, Bank of America, and

Airbnb are proactively thinking about the skills and expertise of their workforce now. These companies and their CEOs are all in the midst of digital transformation and realize that reskilling and upskilling their workforce is a matter of staying relevant. The financial services company Visa, realizing the urgency and strategic nature of skilling its workforce, moved its learning function out of HR and into their corporate strategy division. This means reskilling the workforce is being seen more strategically than just sending people to compliance training. Other companies are creating digital transformation divisions and including learning and reskilling as part of their strategies. These companies are shifting to adapt to the changes in the workforce instead of sticking with the status quo.

Tim Munden, chief learning officer at Unilever, is creating a strategy for upskilling and reskilling more than 161,000 employees around the globe, *not* as part of a separate learning strategy, but as one that is integrated into the company's overall digital transformation strategy. This is a business strategy, not a learning program. Munden believes that "skills are utterly transformational in the twenty-first century. As organizations become networks—networks of people not just employed by you, but networks of people inside and out of the company—skills are what form the connections of the network. Networks form around what a person can do, and we employ people for what they can do, as well as their purpose in doing it."[9]

Developing your employees' skills at a rate equivalent to the rate of change is the key to a sustainable competitive strategy. We need people who have the latest skills and who build new ones quickly. No one knows for sure what skills are going to be needed for the future, so we need a shift in our thinking about learning and skill building too. This means companies need to create an environment where employees are continuously learning new skills: upskilling and reskilling themselves at the same rate that things are changing. Companies can encourage employees to learn every day—learning should be built into the work that they already have, not something that they do separate from work.

The Expert Revolution

Old methods of corporate learning are not going to be effective strategies for building skills for the future. People developing new skills and building expertise are often self-directed. This means employees are learning everywhere all the time, but companies are not recognizing what people are learning, what skills they are building, and how they are working to prepare for their future careers. Your employees are doing this for survival—they want to stay relevant in the workforce too.

You already have lots of experts in your workforce, and we are not just talking about the data scientist, blockchain guru, or AI engineer. We are talking about the woman in the engineering department who is an expert at drafting complex project plans and keeping people working on those projects on schedule. Or the administrative assistant who is an expert at getting urgent purchase orders through the system quickly. Or the software engineer who is a JavaScript expert, highly regarded by other engineers who frequently seek her advice. Or the sales guy who knows how to tell the most compelling product story and give a killer demo. Or the person who knows PowerPoint inside out—and is the first person everyone goes to when they get stuck creating a presentation.

These experts are some of the 80 percent of employees who are not targeted for management or leadership development, who have had to figure out on their own how to develop their expertise and build their skills and knowledge. Driven by passion or curiosity about a specific skill or special interest, they identified what they didn't know and what was new out there. They closed their own skills gap by consuming learning in whatever form they could get their hands on—video, blog, online course, in-person course, book—and applying what they learned on the job until they mastered it. They may have been fortunate enough to have a mentor or a boss who guided their learning journey, but frequently that's not the case.

No doubt, these self-driven experts who can learn quickly are crucial to your company's success, and you need to nurture their ability to build new skills continuously. But to stay genuinely competitive—to grow your talent base—you need to focus on developing new experts, on helping everyone on your team close their personal skills gaps and master specialized capabilities. And the way to do that is by encouraging them to "own" their professional development every day. Rather than dictating from above which skills every employee should learn and how they should learn them, the most effective leaders inspire employees to *personalize* what and how they learn. Humans are wonderfully complex, uniquely autonomous, and ultimately unpredictable. We should celebrate and respect that. And yet, we often try to make everyone the same.

Learning is complicated and messy. It's not enough to offer support to your employees on their learning journey; you also have to create the right environment for employees to take ownership of what and how they learn. The rest of this book will show you how to do just that.

First, we'll review the latest scientific research on how people really learn. Your commitment to helping employees stay competitive for the sake of your business and their careers requires understanding more about what motivates people and how employees can develop expertise. Then, we'll offer seven guiding principles for how you can help your employees build the skills that are so critical to the success of your company, now and in the future. Those principles are:

Make learning a competitive advantage. Company culture plays a critical role in helping employees build skills for the future. Companies that build a culture where learning is part of the overall company strategy— and something that people want and love to do—have a clear advantage. CEOs and business leaders who model this behavior have employees who follow their lead. The best talent wants to work for a company that believes that learning is a priority and that investing in their future is a core value.

Embrace personalized learning. Technology is enabling personalized learning, a key factor in helping people integrate learning with work. People want to learn the skills that will help them succeed, so don't waste their time with what they don't need. Personalized learning enables every person in your company to get the learning they need to build the skills for the next business problem to be solved. We'll talk about how AI and machine learning is helping employees create personalized learning profiles, personalized skill plans, and personalized career pathways.

Combat content overload. We learn from a diversity of sources over the entirety of our lives. We have evolved from a knowledge scarce world to a knowledge abundant world. Excellent learning content is everywhere, and often it's overwhelming to sort through. We'll discuss strategies for using a variety of learning resources—from courses, conferences, certificates, books, podcasts, websites, experiences, journals and articles—to help build expertise. We'll also discuss curated content and machine-curated content and ways to help employees learn what they need, when they need it.

Understand the power of peers. People love to learn from other people, yet we don't always focus on how we can learn from our peers and tap into the knowledge and experience of those who have already mastered a skill. This chapter provides strategies for getting your entire workforce involved in learning from each other and understanding the power of their peers.

Succeed with the right technology. Technology is making new things possible in learning and skill building. In this chapter, we highlight a few education technology companies that are creating new and innovative approaches to workforce learning and putting the learner in the center of the learning ecosystem. We'll also discuss how some of the most forward-thinking companies are creating learning ecosystems that incorporate and integrate a number of best-in-breed technologies to help their companies succeed.

Analyze your employees' skills with data and insights. Learning technologies, search data, and web analytics can produce lots of data about what and how your employees are learning. Using data when creating strategies around reskilling and upskilling your workforce is critical. We'll discuss ways that you can use data to get a better understanding of what skills people have, what they need, and how you can close the gaps. We'll also talk about some of the critical skills needed in the future workplace, and how you can help employees who have built new skills and expertise find the next opportunity in your company.

Make skills and expertise count. Understanding your employees' Skills Quotient, or SQ, is a great way to understand what skills your employees have and what skills they need so they can figure out what they need to do to develop skills for their careers. SQ can also be a valuable tool for companies looking at their workforce as a labor market, with skills being the currency. Imagine what you could do if you had all that data at your fingertips. We'll provide useful case examples describing how you can apply SQ to internal and external recruiting, reskilling, promotions, mentoring, and skills inventory to name a few.

Today, there are more tools, content, and technologies than ever before to help your employees become the experts you need. Above all, success requires that you adopt a new mindset when it comes to skilling your talent, your most important asset. It demands that you start thinking of your employees as complex, unique individuals who should be in control of their own learning and careers. Finally, it dares you to let go of outdated and traditional ways of closing the skills gaps in your workplace and to embrace the new challenges ahead in the expertise economy.

CHAPTER ONE

How We Really Learn

TO HELP PEOPLE become experts—to help them gain knowledge, build skills, and become lifelong learners—it's critical that we understand how adults learn best. Today, we know more than ever about how the human brain works and how people learn most effectively—whether they are trying to gain new knowledge, build a new skill, or change a behavior. For example, we know that sleep has a big impact on how we learn and that mindset and motivation are essential.

In this chapter, we take a jargon-free approach to adult learning theory and explore the latest findings from the science of learning and the related science of motivation. We delve into research on growth and fixed mindsets, and we discover the connection between purpose and learning. We will also discuss what we know about the brain and learning from neuroscientists, while dispelling some myths that are so prevalent today. Resilience, naturally, plays a big part in becoming an expert—we'll look at what science tells us about how people can persevere through setbacks and risk making mistakes, and how they can learn from their mistakes and push self-perceived limits.

Finally, we will explain throughout how current corporate approaches to learning fly in the face of the established scientific research. For example, is your company using primarily instructor-led training with lectures and PowerPoint presentations? Are you killing your employees' motivation by only emphasizing compliance training at your company? Are you telling people exactly what they should learn rather than giving them some autonomy? You probably shouldn't be. We'll show you why and explain how you can apply the psychology and science of learning to help your employees learn and build skills every day until they become true experts, which is so crucial to a company's success.

The Science of Learning

It's surprising that more companies don't use what we know about the science of learning to help their employees learn and build skills. Bror Saxberg[1] has spent his career focusing on the science of learning and advocates putting more "learning engineers" like himself into companies. Saxberg is now leading some of the most forward-thinking learning science strategies for the Chan-Zuckerberg Initiative (CZI) as their vice president of learning science. Founded by Priscilla Chan and Mark Zuckerberg, CZI is a philanthropic investment organization focused on improving equal opportunities and human potential. Education is one of its foundational pillars. Learning engineers can help companies understand the science behind learning and be incredible drivers in getting the most value from employees.

By his own admission, Saxberg sort of fell into learning science as a career. In the late 1970s, he was studying mathematics and electrical engineering at the University of Washington and looking for a summer job. A family friend knew someone who worked for the Jet Propulsion Laboratory (JPL), and Saxberg landed a position at NASA doing communications research. He was asked to come back again the following summer and told to choose a meaningful project to focus on.

The coolest project Saxberg devised was to better understand how the brain stores and codes information. "This was 1978–79—and it was early, so there weren't very many people who were integrating information theory, neuroscience, cognitive science, artificial intelligence, mathematical information theory, and so on. So I just thought—there's really something here."[2]

He completed his studies at the University of Washington, then went on to study at MIT for his masters and PhD, then attended Harvard to get a medical degree (MD). He wanted to cover all the bases in computer science, engineering, and the basic sciences to thoroughly understand how the human brain learns.

He discovered that both cognition and motivation need to be taken into account. According to Saxberg, "Learning is very context sensitive to what's already in your head. You have to understand the cognitive aspects, like what have you already mastered? What is already in your long-term memory? What are your areas of expertise?"

When you realize there is something new you need to learn, Saxberg explains, "you need to start, persist, and put in mental effort. That's when the brain changes. It's like a muscle, and the brain actually changes as a result of learning."

Motivation also plays a big part in effective learning. According to Saxberg, four things can go wrong with learning motivation:

- You don't value what you are doing or how you are doing it
- You don't believe you are capable of learning a complex subject
- You blame environmental circumstances ("I just don't have time to learn")
- You struggle with negative emotional states that distract you from learning—like anger, depression, or distraction

Because of the interrelationship between cognition and motivation, Saxberg emphasizes, "learning has to be personalized according to both the cognitive aspects that you have or don't have and the motivations you have or don't have."[3] For example, if Sarah is pursuing a career in finance, but she hasn't mastered algebra, Sarah is going to have to solve this before she can master finance. That's a cognitive issue.

The truth is that people learn when they care. So how do you get people to care? Saxberg believes that the first step is to understand that each person is comprised of a unique mix of cognitive capabilities and motivations. That means if you expect people to learn, then you need to know what makes them tick from both a cognitive and motivational perspective. Saxberg warns that if you neglect this part of the learning process, "you are going to get what you usually get. And what you usually get in a typical company classroom environment is that most people don't even understand what you are doing; most people just sit around and don't care. Most people just hope to mark this as a fun or interesting session and move on, and there is no discernible impact on their work. They don't start, persist, and put in mental effort."[4] You have to solve for context, personalization, and motivation for successful learning.

Neuromyths about Learning

Despite the amount of knowledge we have about how the brain works in relation to learning, some myths (or neuromyths[5]) have somewhat clouded our thinking about how we learn. According to neuroscientist Julia Sperling,[6] many misconceptions about learning have made their way into the world of work:

MYTH 1: People only use about 10 percent of their brains.
- Reality: You use almost the entire capacity of your brain.

MYTH 2: People are either right-brain thinkers or left-brain thinkers.
- Reality: The left and right parts of the brain do not function completely separately, and learning has nothing to do with the hemispheres of your brain.

MYTH 3: People have an optimal channel (visual, auditory, etc.) through which they learn.
- Reality: People actually use as many channels to learn as they can access. Neuroscientist David Eagleman agrees, and adds that learning is most effective when all of the senses are combined into the learning experience (audio, visual, touch). He reinforces the idea that people learn best when they have to teach someone else how to do something.[7]

MYTH 4: There are certain windows of learning, and when they close, they have no chance of being reopened again.

○ Reality: People can learn new things at any age. The neuroplasticity of the brain allows us to learn, refine, or to add new capabilities all throughout our lives.

The Truth about Learning

So now that we've introduced some of the neuromyths, let's look at the truth about how we learn and what the latest neuroscience research is telling us. Sperling believes there are six things that will help us understand how the brain actually works in regard to learning.[8]

1. We are all capable of learning throughout our lives, and we all have an unlimited capacity to learn.
2. How mindful we are impacts how well we learn something new. Mindfulness (or paying attention to the present moment) and meditation can significantly improve our readiness to take in new knowledge.
3. Mindset matters. If we have a growth mindset, we believe we can learn new things.
4. Focused attention is highly impactful to learning (multitasking is discouraged).
5. We learn best when we have desire. It also helps when we feel learning is relevant to us and when we are in an environment where learning is enjoyable.
6. Positive feedback accelerates the learning journey.

In addition to these six factors, Eagleman also highlights the importance of sleep for effective learning. Eagleman explains that sleep is essential for memory function and for making connections. He says, "Sleep inspires insight and it allows you to synthesize material that you've learned." He also says that pulling an all-nighter, or "cramming," is not a good strategy. It's far more effective to study and then sleep so that the material gets "stitched" into place in the brain.[9]

While cramming may not be the best strategy for learning, reading, in general, *is* important. New neuroscience research[10] reveals that reading fiction, in particular, is good for developing the brain's "theory of mind" and helps people to experience what the main characters are feeling in a story. This builds empathy and the ability to understand mental states, thoughts, emotions, and beliefs. Professionally, it also helps leaders understand their employees and their teams at a deeper level and thus apply more effective motivators based on individual needs.

Learning Fast Doesn't Equal Being Smart

In *The End of Average: How We Succeed in a World that Values Sameness*, author Todd Rose, who directs the Mind, Brain, and Education program at the Harvard Graduate School of Education, argues that people conflate quick learning with intelligence. However, the research shows that in education there is absolutely no correlation between learning fast and being smart.

None.

According to Rose, "We have this view that is so pervasive that fast equals smart."[11] Rose believes it all started with Edward Thorndike and his theories on learning: "He's the one who tried to say there is only one right way to do things, only one path to mastery, and felt intelligence was genetic and should be measured by how fast your brain could form connections."[12] We need to stop this type of "standard" thinking in the workplace.

Standardized testing models are built on this notion (hence the name). They are designed around the principle that an "average" person needs 90 minutes to complete a test, for example. According to Rose, we used to think giving people extra time to complete a test wouldn't make a difference. After all, if you are too slow to finish within 90 minutes, it must mean you aren't bright enough, and therefore will not benefit from the extra time. But for some people, being given more time actually does make a difference.

In fact, slowing down learning overall can work to our advantage. In a study on the perception of speed[13] conducted by psychologist Adam

Alter from New York University, volunteers were asked to respond to a number of questions; some volunteers were given questions written in clear font and others received a more blurred version. It turned out that the people who had to work harder and more slowly from the blurred type gave more accurate responses to the questions than their "speedier" counterparts. The study concurs with Rose's view that thinking fast is not always best.

Rose's work shows that there's more than one way to get something right, there's more than one pathway to mastery, and that taking time to learn is not a sign of poor intelligence. We should celebrate people who pursue excellence and those who choose to learn skills that require time to learn deeply enough to become an expert. Instead we often reward those who succumb to the pressure to do just enough to get the next promotion.

Motivation Is Everything

As stated earlier, encouraging people to learn is also about *motivating* them to learn. Adult educator Malcolm Knowles[14] did the first extensive research on adult learning and found that an adult's strongest motivators are internal (intrinsic) rather than external (extrinsic).[15] Intrinsic motivators are those that come from within and satisfy our natural desires to want to do something; while extrinsic motivation drives us to do something for external rewards, such as money, perks, praise, and so on. In our natural desire to learn, we are more motivated by internal motivators than external ones.

Knowles also discovered that adults need to know *why* they have to learn something. If you want learning to be something that people love to do and not just something that is imposed on them, you have to think about what motivates a person to learn. In fact, when it comes to learning, motivation is the key. In Daniel H. Pink's book *Drive: The Surprising Truth about What Motivates Us*, he describes the science of motivation, believing that for too long "there has been a mismatch between what science knows and what business does."[16]

Pink talks about human motivation in terms of autonomy, mastery, and purpose. He defines these concepts in the following way: autonomy is our desire to be self-directed; mastery is our urge to make progress and get better at what we do; and purpose is our yearning to contribute and to be part of something larger than ourselves.[17] This is similar to management professor Kenneth Thomas' definitions in his book *Intrinsic Motivation at Work: What Really Drives Employee Engagement*, where he identifies intrinsic motivators as meaningfulness, choice, competence, and progress.[18]

These intrinsic motivators are extremely important when it comes to learning and work, yet most companies employ learning and talent strategies that are, in fact, the opposite of what science tells us is most effective. Instead of autonomy and choice, they have a command and control model for telling employees what and when they need to do and learn (including the dreaded compliance training). Instead of mastery and competence, companies appear to be satisfied that employees have completed "training" regardless of whether they have actually learned anything or developed new skills. Instead of understanding that learning and meaningful work contribute to people's need for meaning in their lives, most companies are perplexed when employee engagement rates remain stagnant and 70 percent of employees are just flat out disengaged at work.[19]

The astounding thing is that many companies have not embraced the science and psychology behind motivating people in the workplace. Granted, many tech companies try to engage people through external motivators, but is that really the solution? Companies like Google, LinkedIn, and Facebook famously supply free food, ping-pong tables, onsite massages, and haircuts, among other perks. And while that might appeal to some workers for a while, it doesn't sustainably do anything for long-term loyalty or retention. People don't decide to stay or leave a company based on free food. It's not that those perks are bad (who wouldn't opt for these benefits?), but they don't get to the core reasons people decide to work for or stay with a company long-term. Those motivators are deeper and more intrinsic.

What today's employees want is the ability to have an impact in their work, the flexibility of when and where to do their work, to see their work connected to a bigger purpose, and to have the opportunity to learn and grow in their careers. Compensation is a key external motivator, but recent studies have shown that people, particularly millennials, will take less pay for more flexibility and more opportunities to learn and advance their careers.[20] If companies created strategies to support these findings, they would become more successful, including recruiting and retaining employees. They would also see that today's employees need a sense of meaning and purpose in order to motivate them into learning.

Meaning and Purpose as Drivers for Learning

Many employees want to see their work connected to a larger purpose; they want to feel that they are making a valuable contribution to themselves, their company, and society. As a result, the best employees are often drawn to companies that are mission-driven and want to have a positive impact on society. Aaron Hurst has spent the past few decades researching the relationship between purpose and work.

Hurst founded the nonprofit Taproot Foundation in 2008, whose mission is to lead, mobilize, and engage professionals in pro bono service that drives social change. He then went on to cofound the company Imperative, a start-up that helps people discover and apply purpose at work.

Through his extensive research on how people perceive work, Hurst discovered that people are wired to see work from two different viewpoints. The first is through purpose orientation, meaning that some people view work as a way to gain personal fulfillment as well as a method of serving others. In the second orientation, people view work as a way to achieve status, advancement, and income. Hurst's research shows that out of the 150 million–strong US workforce, there are roughly 42 million people (or 28 percent) who have a purpose orientation. The goal of Hurst's company Imperative is to imagine a workforce where the majority is purpose-oriented, because with this viewpoint at the core, there are huge benefits to employees, companies, and society.[21]

In fact, merging purposeful employees with goal-orientated organizations is a powerful mix. According to organizational psychologist Philip H. Mirvis,[22] when companies are mission-driven and employees are purpose-driven, the combination fosters "developmental engagement where a company aims to activate and develop more fully its employees (and the firm in general) to produce greater value for business and society."

Like Hurst, world-renowned Stanford University psychologist Carol Dweck also agrees that having a purpose makes life more meaningful. Dweck says, "Effort is one of the things that gives meaning to life. Effort means you care about something, that something is important to you and you are willing to work for it. It would be an impoverished existence if you were not willing to value things and commit yourself to working toward them."[23]

Along with being purpose-oriented, Dweck also believes in the power of mindset as a great motivator for successful learning. In her book *Mindset: The New Psychology of Success*,[24] Dweck talks about the power of believing that you can improve. Dweck asserts that people have either a growth mindset or a fixed mindset when it comes to learning. The fixed mindset tells us that we are either smart or not, that we have learned all we can or that we lack the ability to learn a complex topic (like math), while the growth mindset tells us that we have the ability to learn something new every day—even if we're not good (at math) yet, we each have the ability to improve if we try. When scientists measured the electrical activities in the brain between people with both fixed and growth mindsets, they found that people with a growth mindset have connections that are firing like crazy versus those with a fixed mindset whose brains don't engage to the same degree.

Dweck fully believes that when it comes to learning, we should challenge ourselves: "In a growth mindset, challenges are exciting rather than threatening. So rather than thinking, 'Oh, I'm going to reveal my weaknesses,' you say, 'Wow, here's a chance to grow.' If you find yourself afraid of challenges, get yourself into a growth mindset and think about all of the growth potential in following this opportunity, even if it's out of your comfort zone."[25]

When it comes to nurturing lifelong learning, Dweck also believes in the power of "not yet"—a theory inspired by a high school in Chicago that rather than failing students for not passing the course, gave them a "Not Yet" grade instead. As Dweck says, the difference between being told we have failed something and "not yet" is significant: "...if you get a failing grade, you think, I'm nothing, I'm nowhere. But if you get the grade 'Not Yet,' you understand that you're on a learning curve. It gives you a path to the future."[26]

At the university level, some professors naturally use a growth mindset methodology when teaching, meaning that they give students the opportunity to improve before giving them a final grade on a project. In other words, they give them a grade of "Not Yet" and a chance to improve. Let's look at an example.

Cameron took a history class in college on the Vietnam War and was given an assignment to write a paper analyzing three movies that had been made about the war. There were several draft deadlines for the project (several opportunities to practice) and with each draft, Cameron got feedback from the professor, time to reflect, and then an opportunity to make the assignment better. Cameron was gaining knowledge about the Vietnam War, and also developing skills in critical thinking and analysis. Through practice, feedback, and reflection, Cameron made his assignment better with each draft, learning more and more along the way. It's worth mentioning that this steady flow of information and feedback resulted in a positive outcome reinforcing for Cameron 1) the positive experience of writing the paper, 2) instilling a "growth mindset," and 3) reiterating the "Not Yet" grade until Cameron achieved a level of success.

Contrast that to a professor who puts the assignment on the syllabus and offers no chance for direct feedback before the assignment is due. Without practice and feedback, the grade is based on the first and final attempt only. This approach doesn't allow for a true measure of learning ability, nor does it allow for a growth mindset to flourish.

Learning and Mindset as a Competitive Advantage

Companies that understand the power of the growth mindset have a true advantage, not only because they help their employees realize that they should be learning throughout their entire careers, but also because leaders who embrace the growth mindset tend to be more introspective about their own learning and leadership.

Satya Nadella took over as CEO of Microsoft in 2014 and was inspired by the concepts of Dweck. He understands that a learning culture can be a huge competitive advantage: "Culture is something that needs to adapt and change, and you've got to be able to have a learning culture."[27] Nadella embraced Dweck's concepts in *Mindset* and reiterated one of the most important concepts to his employees: "If you take two people, one of them is a learn-it-all and the other one is a know-it-all, the learn-it-all will always trump the know-it-all in the long run, even if they start with less innate capability."[28]

Asking for feedback is not that common for CEOs and can be uncomfortable for leaders who sometimes feel that they need to lead as a "know-it-all." Satya is different and embraces feedback and the growth mindset. He thinks all employees and CEOs should ask themselves at the end of their workday: "Where was I too closed-minded, or where did I not show the right kind of attitude of growth in my own mind? If I can get it right, then we're well on our way to having the culture we aspire to."[29]

Another interesting point Nadella makes is that the employees who are the smartest now may not be the smartest in the long term, depending on their mindset, something that companies should take into account during the hiring process. During the interview process you can identify which people are lifelong learners with the growth mindset; for example, when you ask lifelong learners what they learned the previous year, they tend to respond straight away. When interviewees struggle to answer the question, it reveals that they are not intentionally lifelong learners. People who value learning and can demonstrate learning agility in the workplace are valuable now and will continue to be in-demand talent in the future. And yet, a growth mindset is not the only attribute employees need in today's workforce. As recent research shows, a steady dose of grit goes a long way to optimizing the learning process.

Grit and Resilience

When she was 27 years old, Angela Duckworth left her job in management consulting to teach seventh-graders math in a New York City school. What she discovered during her teaching set her on a path of understanding how people learn and what makes them successful. One of the first things she noticed during her teaching days was that some of her smartest students defined by high IQs weren't doing that well, yet those with lower IQs were some of her strongest performers. It made her realize that there is more to learning than IQ and that motivation played a key factor in her students' ability to learn new things.

After a few years, Duckworth left teaching and became a student again, continuing her journey by doing graduate research, studying psychology and learning at the University of Pennsylvania. She wanted to know more about learning than what could be measured through IQ scores, so she started to ask both children and adults in her studies, "Who is successful here and why?"

In all the studies conducted by Duckworth and her team, in various situations on the job, "one characteristic emerged as a significant predictor of success" and it wasn't social intelligence or IQ; it was grit, or, "passion and perseverance for very long-term goals."[30] Another interesting point about Duckworth's research is that "grit is usually unrelated or even inversely related to measures of talent." This means that when employees' performance is measured at work, rarely do they get rated on their "grit." Duckworth realizes that grit is not the only component of success, but that "hard work does matter." In successful learning, both grit and a growth mindset are two essential elements. But how can we apply these concepts in a practical way?

Getting Practical about Learning

Knowledge and skills are often conflated terms. Consider this example: if you learned Italian (either by taking an in-person class or an online course, by watching some videos, listening to recordings, reading a book, or using a language application) would that mean that by the end of your learning, you would be able to actually speak or write well in Italian? Maybe not. In fact, many people have taken years of a foreign language in formal classes, achieved good grades, and still cannot read or write in the language—they can't do anything with the knowledge they gained. This illustrates the difference between knowledge and skills—you may have gained some knowledge, but you haven't acquired the skill.

In companies today, there is generally no distinction made between knowledge and skills, and everything is thrown into a bucket called "training." Just because you know something doesn't mean you can actually do it. Even if you can do something, it doesn't necessarily mean you are good at it. All it means is that information was communicated in some form with the goal of transferring knowledge. If companies really want to help their employees know more or gain new skills, there has to be a common and basic understanding of what learning is really all about.

Lectures Are Not Learning

In most companies, knowledge transfer is at the foundation of corporate training. Training is usually requested by a leader, a manager, or an employee, and the request often results in lecture-based classroom training or a similar e-learning experience. Some companies assume that the easiest way to resolve a problem is to run a training session rather than take the time to analyze the actual issue.

Say, for example, someone in the team is abusing the remote working guidelines or someone in customer support is getting low customer satisfaction scores. These employees are likely to be sent to some type of "training" based on the misconception that if the employees just knew more, the policies would be followed or the employees could make the customers happier. This type of training is often delivered in the form of a PowerPoint or similar type presentation. The employees passively listen to the information and are even sometimes quizzed, then are supposedly "trained" on the topic. Problem solved?

Recently, in light of rampant sexual harassment and abuse, the US Senate passed mandatory sexual harassment training for senators and their staff. But information is rarely the key to resolving workplace issues. In most cases, the problem has nothing to do with a lack of information. Providing training to an entire group of people to solve a specific problem is like taking away privileges for everyone when only one person is at fault. We often train to the "average" person when in reality there is no "average" person.

This one-size-fits-all approach is simply not effective.

Companies have taken this training approach from the university learning model, but instead of expert professors imparting knowledge through lectures, we have trainers instructing a group or team in the workplace. In school, the students take notes, then use those notes to study for exams, but once the exam is over, for most people, the need to know has passed and a large amount of the knowledge is lost. Students may have gained sufficient knowledge to pass the exam and achieve high scores, but few acquire the necessary skills to apply this knowledge in a practical way.[31] When this model is applied at work, we get similar results. Employees largely forget most of what they learned and rarely apply classroom knowledge to their work on the job.

Medical schools are well known for putting students through hours and hours of lectures, especially during the first years. The amount of information and knowledge that future doctors need to ingest is staggering. A typical medical course begins with a four-year undergraduate degree, followed by four years of medical school, and finally three years of residency. That's eight years of knowledge-building before premed students even get to put their knowledge into practice. The problem is that knowledge only goes so far, and lectures are not the most effective way to learn. It's what you do with the knowledge you gain that is most important.

William Jeffries, Senior Associate Dean for Medical Education at the University of Vermont's Larner College of Medicine, and former advocate for the power of lectures in higher learning, now believes that lectures are *not* the best way to learn. According to Jeffries, "We've seen much evidence in the literature, accumulated in the last decade, that shows that when you do a comparison between lectures and other methods of learning—typically called 'active learning' methods—that lectures are not as efficient or not as successful in allowing students to accumulate knowledge in the same amount of time."[32]

This evidence has encouraged Jeffries and his colleagues to start phasing out lectures in favor of "active learning" (putting knowledge into practice) with a view to rendering lectures obsolete within two years. Active learning involves putting what you know into practice; knowledge is what you know, but skills are what you can do.

Simple Learning Loop

So what is the best method to help employees learn? Whether we want people to gain knowledge or learn new skills, there is a simple "Learning Loop" that everyone goes through if they really want to learn. The Learning Loop is a straightforward way of thinking about the learning process and has four components: knowledge, practice, feedback, and reflection.

Let's use the Learning Loop in the context of building a new skill in the following example. You have an employee, John, who wants to learn how to give a great presentation. First, John needs to obtain some "knowledge" about what it takes to give a great presentation. Being resourceful, John knows he can find knowledge about this skill in a dozen different ways: for example, he could read a book, watch a video, read an article, listen to a podcast, or consume any other content that would help him understand everything he needs to learn about giving a great presentation.

Next, John has to "practice" the skill of giving a presentation. Maybe John practices at home, or with a peer, or in a situation that's not too intimidating. Far too many people skip this step, stopping at the "knowledge" part, but of course this is a mistake. Applying the knowledge

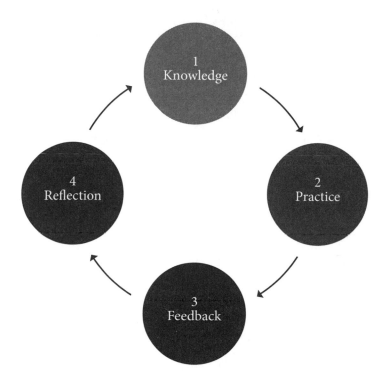

through practice is vital in developing a new skill, and especially important toward getting feedback.

"Feedback" is key to making sure we really understand what we are learning. At this point, John has practiced giving a presentation and now needs some feedback. One way he can get feedback is by practicing in front of a peer, but he could also get feedback through a more formal method. When Kelly was at Yahoo!, the learning organization ran presentation classes where the participants would be videotaped presenting to a group of peers. Afterwards, the participants received feedback in three ways: first, from the instructor (who was highly skilled at giving presentations and providing constructive feedback); second, from their peers in the room; and third, from seeing themselves on video so they could see firsthand how they presented.

Once the participants got the feedback, they were able to "reflect" on what they heard and make modifications to their presentation and delivery. Then they went through the Learning Loop process again. For people speaking or giving presentations on a regular basis, the Learning Loop is less structured but happens nonetheless. They practice, get feedback, reflect, and then make adjustments for the next time.

Let's take another example. Emily is starting a new job at a public relations firm right out of college. In her first week of work, she's learning about her role and familiarizing herself with how everything works in her new work environment. This is the knowledge part of the Learning Loop. Next, she starts to do real work, partnering with more experienced account managers (practice) and maybe sitting in on some client meetings to observe her colleagues in action. During these first weeks, Emily receives feedback from her boss and her peers about her progress. Emily reflects on the feedback, adjusts her actions in real time, and also gains confidence that she is learning and moving in the right direction. It seems so simple, but it is surprising how many people don't get feedback or the opportunity to reflect on that feedback and just hope they are doing okay.

Following each step of the Learning Loop helps us gain and retain important knowledge and skills, while also building a real appetite for further learning.

Reflecting Builds Emotional Intelligence

Reflecting on what you learn is beneficial for so many reasons. It not only creates the environment where you take time to think about your experiences to gain greater insight, but also helps with problem-solving, critical thinking, and emotional intelligence[33] (three of the most important skills for the workplace). It is ideal if you can get feedback to reflect on what you learned, but even in the cases where you don't get immediate feedback after practice, or if you just read a book or an article to gain knowledge, you can still take time to reflect on your own.

This step of reflecting is often one that is missed in the flow of business, and having a structure to catalyze it is critical. Airbnb uses Degreed, which is designed to facilitate lifelong learning and skill development. When their employees complete a learning experience, they can write insights or "takeaways" that get added to their Degreed learning profile. These "takeaways" prompt employees to reflect on what they learned and can then be shared with others and discussed online.

Vulnerability in Learning

Knowing what we know about the brain, motivational drivers, the value of a growth mindset, and the power of grit, why is it that more organizations don't actively apply these principles? One reason is that some people in the workplace don't like to admit that they need to learn new skills because they worry it will make others think less of them. That makes them feel exposed and vulnerable.

This doesn't matter so much in school because we are "supposed" to be learning, and so it seems okay not to know something. But when these same people are not in school anymore and enter the working world, all of the sudden they find themselves in a certain role, but unsure how to apply the knowledge they have learned on the job. How many people do you know who have said they actually know a certain skill even when it turns out they don't? Some people don't want to lose credibility, especially when it comes to being hired or being given new responsibility.

There is a tendency with adult learners to not want to admit that they don't know something or don't have a particular skill. If the boss thinks you don't know how to do your job, will he or she think differently about you? Will it be held against you in a performance review? Even when it's not senior management, employees can get worried about what their peers will say and think. It takes courage to say you don't know something in a competitive work environment. As leaders, we need to understand this and help reassure people that it's okay to not know something. We should be reinforcing the message that everyone should expect to be learning throughout their careers and for the rest of their lives.

Helping people become experts requires a real shift in our own perceptions of what learning really means. This means understanding that each person with whom we work is unique in how they learn. For some people who struggle to learn new things, it could even be as simple as switching their mindset from "I can't" to "not yet."

Five Steps to Helping Employees Learn and Gain Expertise

Now that you know how people learn best, you can think about how to incorporate some of this knowledge into your learning strategies at your company. Here are several ways you can help your employees learn and build expertise:

1. Understand and apply the simple Learning Loop

People learn through this simple process, so make sure all components of the Learning Loop are incorporated into any learning you develop or purchase for your employees. So often companies spend significant money on workplace learning resources from vendors without knowing whether the vendors themselves understand how employees really learn.

2. Model mindset and apply the right motivators

Whenever leaders or employees jump to dictating a "training solution" at your company, step back and ask if that's really the solution to the problem and whether employees will genuinely want or benefit from it. Let employees know that your company prefers "learn-it-all" employees rather than "know-it-all" employees, and make sure leaders and employees model this behavior. Think about the intrinsic motivations of employees, such as autonomy, mastery, and purpose, and let employees take ownership of their own learning.

3. Have employees assess skills gaps

Helping employees understand their strengths, weaknesses, and skills gaps adds incredible value. How do they know what skills they want to build if they don't know where they want to go, the type of skills they need, the skills they have, or the level of those skills? Degreed has added skill assessment and certification as part of its product portfolio to do exactly that.

Another way to think about skills gaps is to "identify the best exemplars."[34] According to business professor Dorothy Leonard, you can ask the following questions to help navigate:

Who is really good at what you want to do?
Which experts are held in high regard by their peers and immediate supervisors?
Whom do you want to emulate?

Then use the answers to assess the gap between you and them. Leonard said, "This requires brutal self-assessment. How much work will this change require, and are you ready to take it on? If you discover the knowledge gap is fairly small, that should give you confidence. If you determine that it's really large, take a deep breath and consider whether you have the courage and resolve to bridge it."[35]

4. Encourage autonomy with your employees.

People really crave autonomy. If you want to provide an environment where employees can be autonomous, it's important to focus more on what work gets done, not how it gets done. Also, build trust with your employees. If you don't trust them to work autonomously, then why hire them?

And finally, give employees ownership over their career trajectory and provide guidance, modeling, and mentorship along the way. Tracy Maylett, CEO of employee engagement consulting firm DecisionWise, says, "Who wants to be told what to do at every turn, and who wants to be the one babysitting? Perhaps there are the few that fit into both of these categories, but that doesn't cut it with good employees—or good managers. That's where balanced and effective autonomy comes into play."[36]

5. Encourage more reading and fewer lectures.

Some of the most well-respected leaders of our time are avid readers. Bill Gates learns new things by reading about 50 books a year.[37] Elon Musk is a voracious reader, saying that the books he read as a child inspired him to build rockets.[38] Mark Zuckerberg made a commitment to read a book every two weeks and shares his reading list on Facebook.[39] And the list goes on: Warren Buffet, Oprah Winfrey, Sheryl Sandberg, and countless entrepreneurs learn through reading.[40] One more tip: stay near and emulate people you admire. Motivational speaker Jim Rohn famously said, "You are the average of the five people you spend the most time with."[41]

CHAPTER TWO

Make Learning a Competitive Advantage

WHEN ANGELA AHRENDTS met with Apple CEO Tim Cook in 2013, it was to persuade him not to hire her. At the time, Ahrendts was the CEO of Burberry and had been instrumental in transforming the very traditional British fashion label (famous for its trench coats) into a hip, fresh brand targeted at a younger demographic. Ahrendts has also been credited with bringing Burberry into the digital age far ahead of its competitors.

When Ahrendts was approached by Cook to come to Apple as part of the retail division, she was flattered but had no desire to leave her job at Burberry. She had worked hard on creating a fantastic working culture and had built strong relationships. During her meeting with Cook, Ahrendts explained to him why she simply wasn't suited to Apple. First, although she had achieved a great deal bringing Burberry into the digital world, she told him she didn't consider herself a technology expert; and second, she told him that despite her long career working for large retailers (before Burberry, she worked for Donna Karan, and Liz Claiborne) she didn't consider herself an expert in retail either. It turned out that Cook's primary interest wasn't in whether she was an expert in either of those areas (even though she arguably was). What Cook wanted was something different. Cook wanted Ahrendts for her leadership skills, her energy, and her values. He wanted her for what she could do for Apple's retail culture.

Cook watched Ahrendts when she gave her 2011 TEDx Talk, *The Power of Human Energy*. During the talk, she described with passion the importance of core values such as trust, intuition, and belief, and how these values, when harnessed, can drive uncommon transformation. One key line convinced Cook for good: "The more technologically advanced our society becomes, the more we need to go back to the basic fundamentals of human communication."[1] From that moment, Cook knew he wanted to hire her. Cook wasn't Ahrendts' only admirer: Sir John Peace, chairman of Burberry and former chairman of Standard Chartered, commented, "She inspires people. And she is the sort of person who wants to see things succeed as a team. It's a rare quality."[2]

The Power of Learning

Ahrendts joined Apple retail in 2014 and has taken a more "human-centric" approach to Apple's culture. In doing so, she is creating an environment that thrives on better communication and supports career development and learning. As an example, Ahrendts wants to move 10 percent of Apple retail employees to other stores around the world to provide more learning and development opportunities.[3] Apple is not the only company to choose this path. Starbucks now offers to pay full tuition for employees to get a bachelor's degree at Arizona State University if they work at least 20 hours a week. This benefits people who wouldn't otherwise be able to pursue a college degree, but it also helps Starbucks reduce the high turnover in its stores.[4] More and more companies are focusing on the power of learning—not only because it benefits employees, but because developing employees just makes good business sense.

Tesla, General Electric, Airbnb, and Goldman Sachs are a few examples of companies that have focused on learning to provide essential development to their leaders, managers, and employees. Aviva, an insurance company in London, has gone one step further in creating an innovation group called "Digital Garage" just to focus on learning and digital transformation for the future.

Other companies would do well to follow their lead. Research from Deloitte shows that high-impact learning organizations (HILOs) achieve three times the profit growth over a four-year period than companies that do not follow a similar approach. Higher management also shows enthusiasm for greater learning: in a Deloitte 2016 Global Human Capital Trends report, 84 percent of executives agreed that learning is an important issue. The report also describes the importance of learning in professional development, in employee engagement, and in building a strong workplace culture.

But it's not just the company executives who want a push for more learning in the workplace. The employees want it too.

Growing evidence shows that companies need to focus on the importance of learning. They need to do this to stay competitive and to attract, engage, and retain their talent. But before companies can successfully implement a learning environment, they need to get the culture right.

Building the Right Culture for Learning

Company culture is multifaceted, and a strong learning culture needs to be a component of an overall healthy company culture. It usually starts with the CEO or leader of a company explicitly expressing the company's vision and mission as well as the values that guide the company's operations. Next, it's up to the leaders and managers of a company to believe in the vision and mission, to communicate it regularly, to explain how employees can impact the mission, and to model behavior that supports the cultural tenants. Then, it's up to the employees to align to the vision and mission, to understand how they can have an impact, and to operate within the values of the company. It's beautiful when it all comes together, and it's a lot more difficult than it sounds.

Organizations known for their innovative corporate cultures include Apple, Google, Netflix, GE, Southwest Airlines, and Zappos, to name just a few. Positive culture makes for a happier workplace, and happy employees equal a healthier bottom line. In fact, studies show that companies with positive workplace cultures are likely to perform better than the competition by an impressive 20 percent.[5] "Authenticity and transparency are key to building a positive and desirable culture—one that will help your company stand out from the competition," said William Arruda, a New York–based personal branding consultant and co-founder of CareerBlast. "Every aspect of the inner workings of an organization must align with the mission, vision, and values of the company."

Cultivating a positive work culture is essential for attracting talent, especially millennials. Millennials, on average, would be willing to forgo almost $8,000 in salary to work in an environment with a culture that was aligned with their values.[6] Gone are the days when salary was at the top of the priority list. These days, job seekers avidly research companies online and study anonymous Glassdoor reviews to gain a deeper insight into different types of cultures and see how they may fit into them. In that sense, millennials are shaping and evolving company culture as we know it.

Company culture is becoming so important that employees often make employment decisions based on the company's culture—either to stay at their current company or to pursue a new opportunity. And that makes sense. People spend a huge amount of their time at work, so all other things being equal, people *should* take time to decide if the culture is a fit. It helps both the company and the employee to ensure there is a good match. Some of the questions employees or potential employees will consider when joining or staying at a company include:

- Am I aligned with the company's vision and mission?
- Am I aligned with the company's values?
- Do I enjoy going to work every day?
- Is the work rewarding and challenging? Can I have an impact?
- Do I enjoy working with my boss and coworkers?
- Do I have the opportunity to learn new skills and develop my career?
- Am I compensated fairly?

The truth is that employees are the company's biggest brand ambassadors, so a strong company culture benefits everyone.

Workplace cultures need to be positive and healthy to incentivize people to continuously learn. When you have leaders who understand and support this, the culture inspires and motivates people who consequently become advocates for the company in a powerful way. Ahrendts is one such leader who believes that the key to Apple's culture lies in its treatment and development of employees. "If you're going to employ people anyway," she says, "why not make them the differentiator? They're not a commodity." As Apple's vice president of retail, Stephanie Fehr, says, "It's just a huge developmental advantage for people here."

"Kick Butt and Have Fun"

Kelly spent a large part of her career at Sun Microsystems, where there was a distinct culture fostered by the very dynamic CEO, Scott McNealy. McNealy led the company for over 25 years, and the consistency in his leadership was one of the reasons the company culture was so powerful.

The company had a collaborative culture where the simple motto was "kick butt and have fun." Employees were loyal and collaborative, and managers were known for being supportive and hands-on when it came to career development. Sun Microsystems was ahead of its time in its focused attention on culture.

Employees were empowered to take risks and be innovative. For example, the now ubiquitous Java programming language was one of its innovations. They were able to work when and where they wanted—a very forward-thinking work-from-home philosophy—and easily move cross-functionally within the company to learn more and build their careers.

Sun's culture was one of empowerment and innovation, and it was a culture that motivated people. Leaders trusted their employees and placed more emphasis on delivering great work than the time spent sitting at a desk. Sun's managers knew early on that if they provided employees with the opportunities to learn, grow, and move along a career path, they would most likely want to stay at the company in the long term—and they were right. Many of Sun's employees stayed for decades, and many of its leaders went on to become CEOs in other companies, including:

- Eric Schmidt, the first CEO of Google and recently departed executive chairman of Google's parent company, Alphabet
- Carol Bartz, former CEO of both Autodesk and Yahoo!
- Satya Nadella, current CEO of Microsoft

So, what happened?

In 2010, Oracle bought Sun and everything changed. The two company cultures were vastly different—where Sun's culture was innovative and employee-centric, Oracle's primarily focused on the bottom line, with employee development coming a distant second. Over time, the culture became more bureaucratic and political and less fun, ultimately catalyzing Kelly and others to leave.

Designing a Company Culture

The Sun/Oracle merger was difficult for many of the former Sun employees because they became part of a larger company with a completely different culture. Acquisitions in general are especially difficult for the employees because the employees end up becoming part of a culture they didn't choose. Typically, when people decide to go to work for a company, they have a choice about whom they work for, and part of their decision is based on the company's culture. So, joining a new company through an acquisition can be good or bad, depending on the acquiring company's culture. Of course, if the culture is not a match, employees can look for career opportunities outside the new company, and many people do just that. Interestingly, studies show that 30 percent of acquisitions fail because of a mismatch in cultures and difficulty integrating the talent.[7]

Organizations that want to maintain their strong company culture need to ensure that everyone understands how the company operates and what is expected of them. The goal for every company should be to ensure that all employees feel part of the culture and at some level feel ownership for upholding and maintaining it. If companies don't define their culture properly, their employees will do it for them. Smaller companies may find it easier to build a strong, positive culture, but when they grow (to over 150 employees), there's always the chance that the company culture will change when new people join, and especially when new leaders come on board.

LinkedIn is a good example of a company that started off small but still managed to maintain its established company culture even as it grew. Kelly experienced this company culture firsthand when she was there. LinkedIn grew from a couple of hundred people in 2009 to just over 9,000 in 2016.[8] During this time, it was recruiting employees from a variety of companies with very different cultures, including Microsoft, Yahoo!, and eBay. How did LinkedIn scale to such a degree and maintain its corporate culture?

First, LinkedIn made the company's values and cultural tenets known from the outset. This was an essential part of the hiring process. In doing so, new managers worked within the LinkedIn cultural expectations, rather than applying what they had inherited from their previous workplaces.

Second, the culture and values were incorporated into everything the company did, from "all-hands" meetings to learning programs and employee evaluations. It was made clear, however, that the values were more than posters on the wall or words that people memorized; they were principles that managers and employees demonstrated by "walking the walk" every day. At LinkedIn, the culture was defined by the leadership, but was lived and embraced day to day by the employees.

A Culture's Guiding Principles

As the LinkedIn example shows, a company needs a clear set of guiding principles to build a strong company culture. These principles determine the type of employee who works there. For instance, in a culture centered on innovation and risk taking, it is no good hiring people who are more process-based and risk averse. They will clash with the culture and likely change it for the worst.

Some organizations would rather employees just leave if they don't prove to be a cultural fit. For instance, online shoe retailer Zappos offers to pay employees to quit if they don't feel comfortable with the company culture. When Amazon acquired Zappos in 2009, it too decided to adopt a similar policy, calling it "pay-to-quit."[9]

Reed Hastings, CEO of Netflix, in conversation with LinkedIn cofounder Reid Hoffman, said that he believes getting the right cultural "fit" is essential to maintaining the corporate culture at Netflix. "I think as a founder if you are trying to build a culture, the first thing you do is you say it is nice to have the right people on your bus, but it is even more critical to keep the wrong people off your bus."[10]

This is why Netflix has a "Culture Deck," which is over 100 pages. Despite new hires having great credentials, they were either leaving or being asked to leave after only a few months because they simply didn't fit into the Netflix culture. The Culture Deck is intended to inform potential applicants what the Netflix culture is all about. It also aims to dissuade people from joining if they don't feel aligned with the company's guiding principles.[11]

However, it would be wrong to lump Netflix in with the Googles, Apples, and Facebooks. The company goes to great lengths in its corporate culture document to emphasize that its culture is pretty far from a Silicon Valley playground: "Our version of the great workplace is not comprised of sushi lunches, great gyms, big offices, or frequent parties. Our version of the great workplace is a dream team in pursuit of ambitious common goals, for which we spend heavily."

Culture is not a consumer good. In Silicon Valley there are companies that serve free catered lunches created by celebrity chefs or some that offer on-site massages. When companies focus on too many "perks," it creates a culture of entitlement, which is a dangerous paradigm because it makes it harder for the company to keep up with the latest trend in perks and doesn't necessarily help your company achieve its goals. Ultimately, culture is not about the extrinsic motivators but more about the intrinsic ones.

David created the culture principles at Degreed not just to lure potential hires but also to help achieve the mission and vision of the company. He believes that people feel valued when they are encouraged to develop their careers. Overall, the people who work at Degreed have joined because the vision, mission, and principles align with their own inherent beliefs and values.

Company Cultures Gone Bad

Not all successful companies have great company cultures. Amazon is still recovering from a *New York Times* article that reported on the brutal way in which employees were treated. According to the article, employees were forced to put their work ahead of their families; had to work 80 hours a week, including evenings, weekends and holidays; and were openly harassed by managers and coworkers.[12]

Similarly, Silicon Valley venture capital firm Kleiner Perkins attracted unwanted media attention when it was sued by one of its employees, Ellen Pao, for gender discrimination. The firm eventually won the lawsuit, but the case exposed a Silicon Valley culture where harassment and discrimination were possibly the norm.[13]

And in 2017, Uber's CEO, Travis Kalanick, was forced to step down as leader of what had become an aggressive, unrestrained, toxic workforce culture. This was further highlighted by former engineer Susan Fowler, who blogged about the sexist culture that was encouraged by Kalanick.[14] This example shows how quickly a culture can deteriorate when the CEO becomes a poor role model or loses focus on the company culture. As Ron Williams, former CEO of healthcare company Aetna, says, "CEOs can go wrong by neglecting the culture. A positive, high-performance culture can quickly turn negative if the CEO is not rigorous in constantly articulating values and holding people accountable for both results and values."[15]

Today, and for the foreseeable future, getting the best talent and being able to keep it is a competitive advantage. When companies get bad media coverage about their company culture, it can drive away top talent and put off potential new candidates.

Different Types of Learning Cultures

Many companies have started to pay attention to the importance of learning and how it can be a huge competitive advantage for attracting and retaining great talent. Josh Bersin, founder of research and advisory services firm Bersin by Deloitte, believes that "reinventing careers and learning is the number two issue in business (followed only by reorganizing the company for digital business)."[16] With that in mind, many companies are wondering how they can create a learning culture.

However, building a culture of learning does not have to be a case of reinventing the wheel. In fact, most companies operate in cultures that already encourage some level of learning or have mastered a mixture of learning cultures. Here are some examples:

1. A culture of compliance training
2. A culture of necessary training
3. A culture of learning
4. A culture of continuous learning

1. A culture of compliance training

Companies with a compliance training culture tend to place a high value on ensuring that their employees adhere to the regulations and requirements necessary to do business.

Many government agencies, financial institutions, airlines, nuclear power stations, and healthcare companies emphasize compliance training because it is required as part of their industry, but that doesn't mean they all do it equally well or can't combine this with other learning. Marc Niemes, director and founder of HealthXN in Melbourne, Australia, has been helping the Australian healthcare industry move beyond just compliance training to one that is focused on building skills and personalized learning. Instead of employees only sitting through uninspiring elearning courses on compliance, healthcare employees are now encouraged to discover learning through various resources, like reading the latest articles in the medical field and listening to podcasts or watching videos on the latest discoveries in the industry.

2. A culture of necessary training

A necessary training culture focuses on teaching employees about highly job-specific tools and processes. This sort of training generally takes place during the onboarding process or when the company is introducing new tools or processes. Successfully onboarding employees has become incredibly important to companies, particularly as studies show that employees form their first impressions of a new company during the first few weeks.[17] This experience often determines whether the employees feel they fit well into the company culture or not. Onboarding 2025 provides a platform for thought leaders to share their successful onboarding strategies with each other. Facebook, for example, asks new engineers to write code to resolve problems on their very first day of work. This method motivates new employees from the beginning, as it gives them real, hands-on experience that directly impacts Facebook's operations in a short period of time.[18]

3. A culture of learning

A learning culture goes beyond compliance and necessary training. This type of culture focuses on building the skills of employees through targeted programs and initiatives. Sometimes the targeted programs are tied to business initiatives, and other times their aim is to develop leadership and management skills. At its core, a culture of learning aligns employee development with organizational goals. Often, the learning is "event-driven," meaning that people are taken out of their jobs to learn new skills, or a company will use a blended approach where they learn both through more structured learning and also on the job.

Airbnb is a good example of a company that has embraced a strong learning culture by providing their employees with an innovative blended learning program for managers and leaders as well as offering them a variety of informal online learning resources for all their employees.

4. A culture of continuous learning

In a culture of continuous learning, learning becomes part of people's everyday work and a regular part of their day. In this way, it becomes a daily habit. People might spend 15 minutes watching a video to build their knowledge on a particular topic, or read an article that helps them think about solving a problem, or they might listen to a podcast on their way to work that will help them do their job better or prepare them for a future role. Work cultures that value continuous learning encourage employees to access YouTube or TED Talks or online courses.

Bank of America is a great example of a company that has created a culture of continuous learning. Employees are encouraged to discover their career passions and goals, and they're empowered to take part in personalized learning and skill building through the career-long learning platform, Degreed. They want their employees to grow and learn and be able to move to different opportunities within the company.

Bank of America also extends learning beyond their employees not only to their customers, but also to the population at large. They partnered with Khan Academy to create bettermoneyhabits.com to help everyone learn about the basics of money, like learning about mortgages and credit scores or whether to rent or buy. They also partnered with Degreed to bring learning resources to active military and veterans to enhance their education, skills, and careers.

Building a Continuous Learning Culture at Degreed

Like LinkedIn and Netflix, creating an excellent corporate culture was one of Degreed's key goals from the beginning. When David cofounded Degreed, he created a "Brand Bible," which outlines the company's mission, vision, and core principles, as a way to help guide employees as they engage in their day-to-day work. Included in the culture section is Degreed's definition of culture: "How we make decisions and treat each other along the journey."

The core principles of Degreed are mission first, balance, equality, empathy, flexibility, dedication, excellence, transparency, and learning.

Definitions of each term in the context of Degreed's mission are highlighted in the guide and then reinforced on a regular basis.

As a learning company armed with a mission to change the way the world learns, continuous learning plays a huge part in the company's culture. First, it provides a way for employees to live the mission and sets a good example for other companies that may want to empower their employees to learn new skills on a continuous basis. Second, learning gives Degreed's employees the opportunity to develop on both a personal and professional level, and grow their careers. This is a major competitive advantage for Degreed, especially when it comes to retention: people tend to stay at companies when they are given the opportunity to develop. To illustrate this point, the engineering team at Degreed has a 98 percent retention rate, which is largely attributed to its culture.

To further incentivize continuous learning, Degreed employees receive $100 a month (or $1,200 a year) to devote to any personal learning activities, including cooking classes or scuba certification. This is distributed through a program called FlexEd, where employees get a preloaded credit card that is tied to their Degreed account. Employees get additional money if the learning relates directly to their role at Degreed. The goal of FlexEd is to foster both personal curiosity and professional development. In return, Degreed has engaged employees and a way to see the learning and skills people are developing.

For example, last year Ryan Seamons, former director of product management at Degreed, spent his FlexEd money in a variety of ways. He really likes to learn through books and found that listening to audiobooks was something he could fit into his busy schedule when he was commuting to work. So Seamons bought a subscription to Audible, an audiobook imprint of Amazon. He also likes to take classes through online university course providers Edx and Coursera, and so he spent some of his money learning through that medium. Seamons also spent some of his FlexEd money on attending a conference in his field, and he spent a good amount of time learning from all the free resources that are now available to anyone with an internet connection.

What would it look like if companies embraced a culture of continuous learning? A culture of continuous learning is an environment where learning is part of everyday work, and where learning is more than compliance or required training. It is a culture where employees can learn in their own time and their own way through accessing all types of both formal and informal learning including videos, articles, podcasts, books, and even attending events. But more than just the myriad learning that surrounds us every day that helps us build skills for now and for the future, learning in a continuous-learning culture becomes something that people love to do and want to do, rather than something they dread. Yet many companies haven't embraced this type of culture. Why? The answer lies in management.

How Managers Impact a Learning Culture

As a manager, when you see an employee watching a YouTube video, do you assume they are goofing off? Do you think they are wasting time? When they see you, do they quickly change their screens to an Excel spreadsheet? If you are a manager or leader who is nodding right now, you could be a *control* manager. In contrast, if you are a manager who views all employees as professionals, as people you hired to get a job done (but you don't really care how they get it done), you are a *power* manager. A power manager is an approachable person with whom employees feel comfortable sharing their ideas.

The corporate workplace is an interesting thing to study. There are a few things that have remained constant during the past several decades. Generally, there is structure, there is hierarchy, there are managers, and there are employees. With these components, everyone is then supposed to contribute to a well-oiled machine for producing services. This model has become outdated in the expertise economy. While the majority of companies still operate this way, it's unlikely sustainable in the long term.

The workplace of the future is more self-directed and autonomous, meaning people can work where, when, and how they want. But, in most companies, there remains a large component of control. Leaders, managers, and HR departments have decided that they know what's best for their employees. To be collaborative, they say, employees need to come into the office every day and work for a certain number of hours during set timelines. Some managers will even tell employees *how* to get their work or learning done, therefore stripping people of the autonomy and creativity to figure out how they could best carry out the tasks.

Kelly worked for a tech company early in her career where the HR manager sat in a window office at the entrance of the building so he could monitor when people arrived and left. This HR manager also made it a habit, along with other managers in the company, to regularly walk around the office and make sure that everyone was working and not socializing. People were generally not very happy working there, and they didn't tend to stay long. Kelly thought that if all tech companies were like this, she was probably not long for the corporate world.

Research on motivation shows us that enforcing "what's best" for employees is not the right way to get the most from them. In fact, people do better when they are given the autonomy to guide themselves. Daniel H. Pink talks more about this phenomenon in *Drive: The Surprising Truth about What Motivates Us*. Pink says that "the secret to performance and satisfaction—at work, at school, and at home—is the deeply human need to direct our lives, to learn and create new things, and to do better by ourselves and our world."[19]

The same concept applies to learning. People cannot be "controlled" into learning what someone else (HR or learning groups) tells them to do. Sure, you can make them sit in a mandatory class or make them click through an online compliance course, but you can't force people to learn. Rather, employees need to figure out what they want to learn themselves and pursue it in their own way. As Pink says, "Autonomy is different from independence. It's not the rugged, go-it-alone, rely-on-nobody individualism of the American cowboy. It means acting with choice—which means we can be both autonomous and happily interdependent with others."[20]

Despite the growing number of innovative companies, it is surprising how many of them still operate from a position of control.

The Illusion of Control

Autonomy is key to getting the most out of employees and encouraging them to learn and innovate. One component of that is allowing people flexibility to work when and where they want. Yet for the most part, companies like Google, Facebook, LinkedIn, and Apple prefer their employees to come into the office every day because it fosters in-person collaboration.

But how collaborative can employees be in such a huge working environment? Some of these tech companies, like Google, Apple, Facebook, SAP, and Oracle, are made up of dozens of buildings in a single campus. These companies have expanded so much that people have to drive to these buildings to have meetings with coworkers. So what happens in these types of organizations is that employees spend hours commuting to work only to use video conferencing to collaborate with people who work in a different building. Why force people to commute to work if they are going to use technology to collaborate in any case? Arguably, the reason has its foundation in control.

Kelly worked at Yahoo! for a few years at a time when the company was struggling. In two years, there were five CEOs, which was unsettling for people who worked there. While the leaders and managers were playing musical chairs and changing the vision and the strategy of the company every six months, the employees were going through a hard time too. People had difficulties focusing, and there was a sense that what they were working on might not matter to the next person in charge. Yet one of the great things about Yahoo! was the flexible work. People could work remotely if their manager approved, and employees were given some sense of autonomy.

But here was the kicker—getting permission to work from home depended on the type of manager. The control managers wanted to see their teams in the office every day, but the power managers were happy to approve a more flexible option. As there were no guidelines from the top, and no consistent message delivered about remote working, there was a lot of confusion among employees about who could do what.

For instance, one of the leaders of the Product division of Yahoo! was getting frustrated by the lack of deliverables in his organization, and he blamed remote working. One day he took a picture of the number of cars in the parking lot on a Friday (there weren't many). He sent that picture to everyone in the division with a comment implying that the absence of cars in the parking lot meant that very little work was being done that day. Ironically, this company also had buses shuttling people to work every day to relieve them of the stress of a bad commute. While it's great to see people energized and working together in the office to innovate and solve problems, just because you don't see it doesn't mean it's not happening.

When Marissa Meyer became CEO in 2012, she got word that people were taking advantage of the remote-working environment at Yahoo! In a decision that was widely debated in the media and throughout the industry, Meyer decided to ban all working from home.[21] That resulted in a lot of talented people leaving the company, since autonomy and flexibility were highly valued by those employees. To be fair, there probably were a lot of employees taking advantage of the remote-working situation at Yahoo!, but ultimately the managers should have been held accountable for the people who worked for them. Perhaps then the situation might have unfolded differently.

Autonomy and flexibility only work if managers frequently connect with their employees to discuss tasks, set goals, set expectations, and provide feedback. If a remote-working situation isn't working out, surely the manager should take accountability for the employee's failure to deliver. Then they have a choice to make: either have a proper discussion to ascertain the reasons why they are struggling, or fire the employee. After all, if managers don't trust their employees to work remotely, why hire them at all? If managers took the time to discuss goals and deliverables with their teams, then they wouldn't need to care so much about when and where they worked. But let's face it, it is harder and more time-consuming to engage with employees on this level. Research shows that managers don't like to give feedback, especially negative feedback, which leads to lack of engagement with their employees. Instead, many managers measure productivity by how much time their employees spend in the office.

Why foster an environment of control at all? How about, instead, transforming these controlling cultures into ones that empower creative, innovative, smart people who are given the freedom and autonomy to work in a way that makes them most productive and allows them to learn and develop along the way? That's the key to really creating a company culture that puts autonomy and learning at its core to get the best of what people can achieve.

Degreed is one of the companies that is creating the workforce of the future. Although Degreed has three offices—headquarters in San Francisco, another office in Salt Lake City, and an office in Leiden, Netherlands—it also has people working from home all over the world. Employees can work anywhere at any time and have autonomy in where, how, and when they do their work. There are weekly company video meetings that help people connect and communicate, and every physical office fosters collaboration in innovative ways.

For example, in the office in Leiden, the team agrees to come into the physical office Tuesdays and Thursdays, but doing so is not mandatory. Why is it not mandatory? Because giving people an option provides them with a sense of autonomy, a sense of choice. It drives motivation, but also, interestingly, it instills a sense of accountability to their coworkers. They feel accountable to each other to come into the office on those days because it's coming from each other and not the top down. Companies that build a learning culture that provides real autonomy and flexibility in the workplace will attract the best and most creative people. And happy, motivated employees lead to greater benefits to organizations, including higher retention, increased productivity, and higher motivation.

The New Employer/Employee Relationship

The workforce will continue to evolve and change the way we think about company culture. In Reid Hoffman's book *The Alliance,* he describes a new employer-employee relationship emerging in the workplace. While people are certainly changing jobs more often than they used to, Hoffman believes that managers and employees need to be more upfront about what they expect from their working relationship regardless how long it lasts. He describes this new employee-employer relationship as an alliance, "a mutually beneficial deal, with explicit terms, between independent players. This employment alliance provides the framework managers and employees need for the trust and investment to build powerful businesses and careers."[22]

Kelly and many leaders at LinkedIn started using this model with their employees, and it aligns very well with the notion of the power manager we described earlier. When a new employee starts a job, they have a conversation with their manager about how long they will realistically be in that role. It might be a two- or three-year "stint" or as Hoffman calls it, a "tour of duty." During that time, the employee is expected to give 110 percent to this job, and in return, LinkedIn promises to help build skills necessary for career development. Over the course of the tour, both manager and employee discuss progress and milestones, and when the project comes to an end, there will be another discussion regarding next steps. The tour usually ends with the employee taking on another assignment, which could be either inside or outside the company.

For example, at LinkedIn, Kelly managed one of the leaders in her organization (we'll call her Julie) who was on a "tour of duty." They had a great partnership and very open conversations about Julie's career aspirations. Kelly promoted Julie at the end of the first tour and started her on a second. About halfway through the second tour, Julie got an opportunity to lead an entire learning organization at another tech company. Julie came to Kelly and asked for her advice. While Kelly was disappointed to lose Julie, she knew that the next logical career move for Julie was outside of the company and supported her wholeheartedly.

This is a great example of how the new employee/employer relationship can work. In most companies, when employees haven't been given much guidance, they start looking for new opportunities externally and often give notice before they've even had the discussion with their manager. However, Julie felt comfortable enough to come to Kelly and discuss her new opportunity before Julie committed to the other job. This gave Kelly the chance to offer Julie alternative roles at LinkedIn and encourage her to stay. In this case, it made more sense for Julie to leave. However, because of their openness with each other, their relationship remains strong. By retaining that strong relationship, they keep the door open to working together again in the future and keep networking opportunities alive. At many companies, there are many "boomerang" employees— people who've left on good terms, but later returned. In these situations, even when employees leave, they are likely to recommend your company as an amazing place to work, especially when they have come from an environment where respect, trust, and open communication are woven into the company culture.

How to Create a Culture of Continuous Learning

Once you have built a positive culture designed to encourage autonomy and self-direction, you can start to develop the concept of continuous learning in your workplace. Here are several ways to cultivate this learning environment:

1. Think about the type of learning organization you want

Think about how you can make learning something people love to do rather than something they dread. Many companies fall into the trap of dictating the type of learning methods for their employees based only on what the company needs. This is why there are so many cultures of compliance training and necessary training. Instead, employees really want to grow and develop in their careers. People have a natural desire to learn, and we need to enable, nurture, and encourage that.

What kind of skills do they want to develop? How do they want to learn? Engaging your employees and bringing them into the discussion will encourage them to embrace further learning.

2. Communicate, communicate, communicate

If your employees don't know about your organization's commitment to continuous learning, then how do you expect them to engage with it? Make sure the message is embedded not only in your company's mission, vision, and values, but also in everything you do, so that everyone is fully aware that learning is entrenched in your culture.

Perhaps even more importantly, make sure that as leaders and managers you are modeling and communicating the value of learning by consistently building your own skills. If your employees see their leaders and managers actively encouraging learning and taking part in their own skills development, then this will eventually become part of the culture.

3. Provide your employees with the learning resources they need

It may sound obvious, but make sure you equip your employees with the resources they need, including money to get learning on their own if possible. These resources may come in the form of online courses, subscriptions to audiobooks, access to podcasts, or a video learning library. Show support by giving them dedicated time during the working day to learn. It's no use expecting employees to learn new skills when they are constantly at the mercy of their daily tasks.

4. Understand employees' career goals

For learning to be effective, it needs to be connected to employees' career goals. Managers need to check in with their employees regularly to gain a better understanding of their career goals, strengths, areas for development, and the short- or long-terms goals they want to achieve. Regular check-ins provide employees with the motivation to stay on track and complete their learning and career goals. But remember to be a power manager and not a control manager. Most employees prefer a little guidance or coaching over more directive instructions. Technology can also provide transparency and guidance into career goals. For example, Pirelli, the Italian tire company, is using a professional development platform, Growithus,[23] to help guide their employees on their career goals, and both Bank of America and Unilever are using Degreed for their employees to set career goals and map learning to skills, then map skills to careers.

5. Relate learning goals to the bigger picture

Take time to explain to employees why learning is so important. It needs to make sense for them on a personal level and on a company level. How will their learning impact their personal career path? And how does it contribute to organizational goals and the vision and mission of the company? Once employees have a sense of the meaning and direct influence of their own learning, they will be more invested in achieving organizational goals.

6. Make sure to follow up

Studies show that the most successful companies are 73 percent more likely to follow up with their employees after they have completed a learning activity.[24] This discussion might involve asking your employees what they thought of the activity (good and bad), if it met their expectations, and how they could apply this new learning to their roles. Without this follow-up, employees will likely forget what they've learned after a few months and consequently fail to apply their new knowledge on the job.

There is a huge difference between dictating what someone should learn and taking an active interest in their career development. Ongoing communication is incredibly important, so you should have both ongoing career discussions with your employees as well as conversations about specific learning activities and skills they are building. This is how you can support them as a manager.

CHAPTER THREE

Embrace Personalized Learning

ERSONALIZATION IS EVERYWHERE. In the past several years, countless software apps have been created to personalize your daily experiences. Spotify lets you personalize your own playlists and suggests
new music you might like; Netflix makes movie suggestions targeted
just for you; you can track your food consumption and measure your
weight changes based on your personal goals using MyFitnessPal; and
the Headspace app lets you select individualized meditations based on
your schedule, your mood, and your level of experience. Because these
apps are targeted to personal needs, they not only increase your levels
of engagement, but also enhance your overall experiences—they are tailored just for you. Personalization, however, goes well beyond our life-
style activities. It also plays a key role in learning.

A study carried out by the Brandon Hall Group found that 90 percent of companies believe that personalized learning promotes personal
development, and 93 percent agree that it helps people reach their goals
more effectively. Despite this overwhelming response in favor of personalized learning, fewer than 50 percent of the companies surveyed admitted to implementing it in the workplace.[1]

If the goal in corporate education is to move away from a
one-size-fits-all mentality, then we, too, must embrace personalization in
learning. This means we should provide learning that is customized for
an individual based on their skills and knowledge gaps, their personal

and professional goals, their milestones, and their specific interests. It's the type of learning that helps people succeed.

To help people achieve their goals within your company, you must tailor their development to their goals or risk top performers leaving in search of companies that will nurture their learning. Consider a 2015 Gallup survey that found that "when 93 percent of Americans advanced in their careers, it was by taking a job at another company."[2] This illustrates that people need to be given the opportunity and the support to learn on the job—especially if employers want to keep top talent for the long term.

The Old Standard

Companies have consistently struggled to implement personalized learning experiences that can help their employees build skills and advance careers. The reasons lie in historical work practices and their influence on education. To really embrace the notion of personalized learning, we need to understand how work has evolved. A huge proportion of employees in the workforce today are now knowledge workers, not factory workers. Since 1980, employment in jobs requiring stronger social skills, namely interpersonal, communications, or management skills, increased from 49 million to 90 million, or 83 percent. Further, employment increased 77 percent (from 49 million to 86 million) in jobs requiring higher levels of analytical skills, including critical thinking and computer use.

That means that the standardized work and education systems companies have used for decades are outdated. While Fredrick Taylor's scientific management approach improved work efficiencies, productivity, and output during the Industrial Revolution, it no longer applies. The goals for our workforce in the knowledge and expertise economy have shifted. Successful companies today focus on how they can find, develop, and nurture the best talent in the most personalized and relevant way possible.

There Is No "Average"

The education system we have today was designed for a different time—it was developed for the industrial era, when the majority of people worked in factories and the goal was efficiency. Todd Rose, director of the Mind, Brain, and Education graduate program at Harvard, believes that companies and schools are hampered from implementing personalized learning because of outdated theories originating from the standardized models implemented during this industrial age. He says, "Many of our existing assumptions about education are based on a highly constraining notion of 'average-based' approaches to understanding individual learners. Every day we are measured against a fictional 'average person,' judged according to how closely we resemble the average—or how far we exceed it."[3]

Corporate training is often modeled on the notion of the "standard" or "average" person; but, according to Rose, there is no such thing as an average person, an average education, or even a standard way that people learn. Companies need to move away from the one-size-fits-all, standardized learning model and personalize every single employee's learning experience. For learning to succeed, it has to take place on the individual level.

We have to adopt a mindset that trusts the intelligence and potential of our employees and puts them at the center. You must think of them as your learning "customer." We don't need to impose artificial limits on them or treat them as if they aren't capable. If employees aren't learning and building skills based on their personal goals and skills gaps, both companies and individuals lose. Companies need to start empowering their employees and understand that employees should be driving the conversation around learning.

Standard Career Paths

Rose also believes that companies need to rethink the idea that they can control the career path of their employees because there is no such thing as a standard career path. To support this point, he refers to the science of equifinality, the principle that there are multiple ways to achieve successful outcomes. Rose adds, "There's never just one way to get there. This isn't true just for learning and careers, this is true in biology and in the brain; it's a mathematical fact that there cannot just be one optimal path."[4]

Rose is a good example of someone who has followed a unique and interesting career path. By his admission, he wasn't a strong student and dropped out of high school. He worked several minimum-wage jobs before getting his GED credential and eventually his undergraduate degree by attending night classes at a local college. Yet today, he's a Harvard professor. Most would define his journey as unconventional to say the least, but he still got there.

Kelly's career path also would be considered outside the supposed "standard." She started as an English major in college, worked in tech companies developing online help systems, moved into product development, then to corporate strategy doing acquisition integration, and finally to leading corporate learning. When a friend asked her one day, "If I want to get into your field, can you tell me what path you took so I can do the same?" Kelly told her friend that her career path was something she could never have predicted. Kelly embraced new challenges and opportunities and emphasized that the road to the right career often involves many detours along the way. It's the rare person who has a standard career path.

Learning through Experience

The fact is that organizations rarely allow for natural, organic learning— learning based on life experiences for which we don't get any credit. Many companies will benchmark employees higher if they have an MBA, but they don't take into account the real-life learning others have built over years of practice and mastery.

Earlier in Kelly's career, she led the acquisition integration organization at Sun Microsystems. This meant that whenever Sun acquired a company, she and her team were responsible for successfully integrating all the new people and functions into the business. If the company had a sales organization, her team created a strategy for merging the two sales groups. Engineering, IT, Customer Support, Marketing, Finance, and HR all needed integration strategies to merge people, processes, and technology. After doing the job for two years, Kelly thought maybe she should go back to school and get her MBA. She was surrounded by dozens of business and legal professionals who all had MBAs or law degrees from prestigious universities, and she felt she needed some professional validation. Doing the job and getting promoted while doing it somehow didn't seem enough.

Kelly went to her C-suite boss and had the conversation with him, and to her surprise he thought the idea was crazy. He told her that if she went back to school to get her MBA, she would be sitting in a classroom listening to case studies of company acquisitions rather than actually working on them. Kelly was getting on-the-job experience that most MBA students were only studying out of books, and she had the added advantage of learning from her peers and being supported firsthand by experienced mentors and coaches. It turns out that sometimes the best way to learn is just to jump in and do something, try new things, and learn from mistakes.

A Personalized Approach to Education

Dale Stephens, founder of the social movement UnCollege and author of *Hacking Your Education*,[5] knows better than most that there is no such thing as a conventional career path. Stephens argues that Americans are paying way too much for a college education and are learning too little.[6]

UnCollege helps people prepare for the future by taking control and ownership of their own education through personalized learning and by focusing on developing skills like problem solving, creativity, and critical thinking in nontraditional environments. Some people prefer learning in a more traditional college structure, but others want something different. For those people, instead of sitting in a classroom, UnCollege focuses on providing mentors, giving students hands-on experience around the world, and instructing them in how to take advantage of the wealth of resources available to them.

Laurie Pickard, author of *Don't Pay for Your MBA: The Faster, Cheaper, Better Way to Get the Business Education You Need*,[7] is another pioneer in personalized, online education. She founded the No-Pay MBA website and pieced together a business education while working abroad. She realized that for the cost and time required to get an MBA, she could access many of the same courses she would take via online MOOC providers and decided to build her own two-year curriculum. Her journey also shows how you can customize and personalize your own education, and that you don't need to adhere to standardized models.

While organizations like UnCollege and No-Pay MBA are use cases of personalized learning, many schools and companies still resist. This is partly due to different interpretations of what personalized learning means. For example, one school in Arizona envisioned a personalized learning model featuring a technology-driven approach.[8] It left learners alone in front of computer screens in small cubicles where they were largely cut off from teachers and peers. Although their test scores rose, the program was discarded when enrollment dropped off. It turned out that students were not attracted to a school that isolated them in cubicles for long periods of time.

Rose argues that "a well-designed and executed personalized learning model can enhance teacher-student interaction. Students learning in isolation, interacting with only a computer, should never be the result." He says, "It's about freeing up more time for the high-value relationships between the teacher and the student and [between] that student with other students. You can best facilitate those deep social interactions by having a system that understands each person as an individual and is responsive to that."[9]

There is a common fear that using learning technology will do away with the need for teachers and instructors, but the reality is that when it comes to personalized learning in schools and organizations, community is essential and teaching professionals will be needed more than ever. The Gates Foundation, which focuses on advancing education, agrees and says, "In personalized learning, the student is the leader, and the teacher is the activator and advisor."[10]

One of the main goals of personalized learning is ultimately to combine the best of what the ecosystem has to offer. It's not an either/or proposition, but rather aims to unite the best features of learner motivation, technology, and online learning supported by teacher and peer expertise. The student or employee may access the knowledge online, but they still need their teachers and peers in-person so they can practice and solve problems. Technology plays a key part, but as Rose says, "The solution is not to simply take an old existing model and problem and put it online—for instance, taking a lecture-based class, videotaping it, and then putting it online is not the solution!"[11]

The foundation of the personalized learning approach always requires some human touch. One-size-fits-all classes, standard career paths, and systematic performance ratings are all part of an antiquated system that needs to be transformed into one that champions personalized learning. The problem is that even data-driven companies that have the necessary resources, according to Rose, "aren't using the data to help them personalize their employees' workplace experiences." We have an incredible opportunity to change the paradigm.

Rose stresses that to really transform the antiquated systems, we need "to get to some of these enlightened CEOs and say look, I know it's scary, but at the end of the day, your bottom line is about finding and developing more talent, more diverse kinds of talent, more experts, and genuinely be a learning organization. I don't think anyone would disagree that that's a really good outcome. There is an enormous 'first mover' advantage here. If you get this right as a company, your ability to develop in-house talent will be second to none."[12]

Personalized learning in action

For personalized learning to succeed, the company must support it and create an environment where the employee can succeed. While employees need to take responsibility for their learning and career development, managers should provide feedback, advice, and guidance.

You could argue that self-motivated employees take learning into their own hands even without managerial support or personalized technology to help them. But if you ask most people what they learned last year, not many could answer that question. That's where personalized learning records or profiles come in—to help people keep track of all the valuable learning they do every day. Ultimately, you want learning to count for something toward your goals.

Let's take the example of Rico Rodriguez,[13] a 30-year-old software developer and learning enthusiast who learned how to code through self-directed, personalized learning. Rico studied neuroscience at Yale but decided against a career in neuroscience. Instead, he took a job as a sales rep at eLearning company Moodlerooms straight out of college. That led him to his next role, as a sales effectiveness associate in the Offers group at Google, where he helped sales reps generate consistent, high-quality leads.

While Rico was coaching sales reps, he realized there was a limitation in Google Spreadsheets that made it difficult to carry out some of the analysis requested by managers, so he started thinking about a solution. He decided he would learn how to code, beginning with the Python programming language. But he also felt he needed a mentor to help advise him, so he found someone at Google whom he respected and was willing to give him some guidance around learning this new skill. Once Rico learned Python, he suggested to his manager that he apply his new skill to a project that the engineers didn't have the bandwidth for: a calculator app that Google sales reps could use to replace the cumbersome spreadsheets. Rico's manager agreed to let him work on the project and so Rico moved from sales to software development.

Knowledge workers like Rico tend to take learning into their own hands to direct their career trajectory. But this is rarely done entirely in isolation. Two important factors impacted Rico's motivation and determination to move into software development. First, he had a manager who believed in him and his ability to learn new things, a manager who gave him the opportunity to do something new—in this case build the calculator application for the sales team. Second, he found a mentor who gave him guidance about how his learning was progressing. Sometimes a manager can be both role model and mentor, but other times different people take on each role. Overall, for personalized learning to work, the learner must be the person driving the goal, the manager should support it, and a mentor can help guide progress and provide feedback.

However, even with support, people must be motivated to learn in the first place. For example, nobody told Rico to learn to code in Python—he set his own goal and created a challenge that motivated him. From there, he followed the path toward personalized learning. It is impossible for any meaningful learning to take place without that initial self-drive and self-motivation, and there is no better way to learn than applying new skills directly to real work. After he set his personal goal, Rico identified a mentor who could give him feedback on the work he produced. Ultimately, Rico discovered learning resources that were available to him around coding (both online and in person), carved out time to learn, and started developing the application as he was learning how to code.

Rico reflected on the feedback from his mentor, made a lot of mistakes, and through trial and error learned how to program in Python. Because his learning was personalized based on his professional goals and his skills gaps, he was able to develop a successful application at Google that helped solve a real business problem.

After Rico spent a few years at Google, Kelly hired him at LinkedIn to work on a learning technology platform. She found that his skills in both coding and neuroscience were a great combination when applied to a platform that focused on personalized, social learning. But his technical skills were not the only reason for Kelly's decision to hire him. Rico was also curious, had great learning agility, and took personal responsibility for his learning and career development—exactly the type of attributes that would put him on a successful career path.

For the next phase of Rico's career journey, he's decided that he wants to learn more about data science, one of the top skills many knowledge workers consider important for the future. Data science helps people explore data in various forms and extract meaningful knowledge and insights. As in his approach toward coding in Python, Rico's approach will use personalized learning and a variety of learning resources, including an expert or mentor in the field to guide him. As Rico's experiences show, it takes a combination of motivation, mentors, and learning resources for successful personalized learning to happen.

Learning Agility

One of Rico's stand-out attributes is his learning agility. Today, companies need agile learners to solve the problems they haven't even figured out they have yet. After all, would you rather hire an employee who is genuinely curious and wants to learn and build new skills, or an employee who needs to be told what to do and just wants to get through the working day? While employers have a role to play in helping employees learn and prepare for the future, when it comes to hiring, they would do well to recruit people based on their curiosity and desire to learn.

In fact, learning agility is, and will continue to be, one of the most desirable skills for the future. Rose believes that organizations can make giant costly mistakes when they don't pay enough attention to the types of employees they recruit. "The cost of being wrong when you hire people is incredible: the turnover and the hiring and the onboarding, alone. It's such a waste. If we can provide a far more nuanced and accurate picture of the kind of skilled person that you want for that job, life gets a lot better for you as a company. And if you apply those same principles to how you become a learning organization, then you're really getting somewhere."[14]

Let's look at the case of Cameron Rogers, another example of learning agility. When Rogers was studying public relations and marketing at the University of Oregon, he happened to meet the CEO of a small Silicon Valley training company at a social gathering who desperately needed a social media marketing strategy. When the CEO discovered Cameron was studying this subject in school, he offered him the chance to do a summer internship at his company. While Cameron was thrilled to be offered such a fantastic opportunity, he was also apprehensive. He felt confident in his knowledge of social media tools such as Twitter, LinkedIn, and Facebook, but he had never created a marketing strategy using these tools for a real company before. Even more unnerving was the fact that he wasn't scheduled to take a social media marketing course at his university until the fall quarter—after the internship was over.

Nevertheless, Cameron was motivated to figure out how he could learn to create a social media strategy so he could succeed in the internship. Fortunately, the University of Oregon provides a wealth of online resources for their students. He tapped into his community at school, did some research, and also found several online resources. In particular, he used an online course by Guy Kawasaki—"How to Rock Social Media"[15]—as well as another Lynda.com course on "Marketing Foundations: Social Media."[16] The CEO turned out to be a great mentor as well and gave Cameron feedback throughout the internship. After several iterations, continued learning, and relevant feedback, the project was delivered to the CEO's satisfaction.

This self-directed, personalized approach to learning turned out to be the key to Cameron's success. Thanks to his school and online resources, he found exactly the learning he needed to fill his own skills gaps. He acquired new skills he was also able to put into practice immediately in a real company, and he gained valuable experience that he could put on his resume and LinkedIn profile. This real-life on-the-job experience put Cameron ahead of the game when the social media marketing class came around in the fall. The initiative and learning agility that Cameron demonstrated illustrates the employee who will thrive in future corporate environments.

Online retailer eBay looks for employees like Cameron. It hires employees who demonstrate learning agility, and it also promotes personalized learning and career development strategy within its staff once they're hired, which has proved to be incredibly successful.

When eBay introduced its new learning philosophy worldwide to all its employees, the company made it clear that all employees were responsible for their own career development. Employees were, however, reassured that they weren't on their own entirely and would be equipped with the relevant tools, guidance, and help along the way. Here are the four important components to eBay's learning strategy for career development and personalized learning:

- Career exploration
- Learning and skill building
- Applying new skills on the job
- Communicating career success stories

Let's explore each one in more detail.

Step 1: Career exploration

First, eBay employees are asked to think about their career aspirations, a method designed to encourage self-exploration. To facilitate the process, they are provided with a tool called Fuel50, which uses a Career Navigator product, to reflect, explore, and plan their career journey. This tool is designed to dive into employees' motivations and interests. For example, employees are asked questions like, "What's important to you?" and "What do you value as a person and as an employee?" It also helps to define talents and identify the skills employees would like to use more and skills they would like to develop. This career exploration phase is a great starting place for employees to frame the "big picture" of who they are, what they want, and where they want to go with their careers.

Step 2: Learning and skill building

Once employees have completed the career exploration phase, they use Degreed to decide what skills they want to focus on—they can even target a particular role with required skills attached to the role—and start building a skill plan. They can then use the product to self-assess against the skills they selected and have their manager and peers assess them on those skills as well. Once they have a good sense of the skills they need to focus on, Degreed then populates their learning plan with curated learning content in the form of learning pathways. Curated content in these learning pathways includes such content as videos, books, podcasts, in-person courses, and on-the-job learning experiences. Degreed then shows progress against employees' learning and adds skills to their personal learning profile as they build them.

Step 3: Applying new skills on the job

When employees have built new skills, they can then match their new skills to real job and project opportunities through an internal career marketplace, which was built in partnership with Rallyteam and their technology. eBay has the right idea: providing employees with opportunities to apply their skills is critically important; if employees build new skills but can't apply them, the learning can be lost. When this happens, employees lose motivation and may look outside the company for a place to apply their new skills. Helping employees find opportunities to advance and grow inside the company is an essential part of eBay's learning strategy. A unique component of this strategy is enabling employees to keep their current role while taking time to work on a different project for a set time. For example, say an employee learned project management as a new skill. They can go onto the career marketplace and find a project to apply that skill and gain important real-work experience.

Step 4: Communicating career success stories

The last part of the program at eBay is about connecting with others. The company set up a marketing campaign and website where employees can share their personal career journeys at eBay, network with others, and participate in communities to share their learning experiences.

The "Brilliant" Personalized Learning Philosophy

Brilliant.org[17] is an online community for students and professionals that focuses on personalized learning for topics related to math and science. The co-founder and CEO, Sue Khim, featured in the 2012 *Forbes* list of "30 under 30 in Education" created the company when she was just 26.

Math professors, scientists, and other technical minds propose difficult problems and challenges to be solved by students. Students are also given new problems to solve based on their past performance and permitted to move at their own pace. The next stage is to share their answers and problem-solving methods with the Brilliant.org community. The principles promoted by Brilliant.org align well with the philosophy we've outlined in this book and with our approach to personalized learning. Here are some useful guidelines from Brilliant.org to share with your employees in relation to a more personalized learning experience:

Effective math and science learning...

1 **Excites.**
The greatest challenges to education are disinterest and apathy.

2 **Cultivates curiosity.**
Questions that cultivate natural curiosity are better than the threat of a test.

3 **Is active.**
Effective learning is active, not passive. Watching a video is not enough.

4 **Is applicable.**
Use it or lose it: it is essential to apply what you're learning as you learn it.

5 **Is community driven.**
A community that challenges and inspires you is invaluable.

6 **Doesn't discriminate.**
Your age, country, and gender don't determine what you are capable of learning.

7 **Allows for failure.**
The best learners allow themselves to make many mistakes along their journey.

8 **Sparks questions.**
The culmination of a great education isn't knowing all the answers—it's knowing what to ask.

Technology for Personalized Learning

Technology can play a key role in helping your employees embrace personalized learning. Chapter 6 elaborates more broadly on how you can succeed with the right technology, but it's worth noting here that Degreed is an excellent example of technology that enables personalized learning. Degreed is a learning platform that puts the learner in the center of the learning experience. It allows individuals and companies to discover learning, to build skills, and to take a "record" of their personalized learning with them no matter where they go in their career. Organizations that provide technology to enable personalized learning not only make it easier for their employees to build skills, but also make learning more meaningful. Employees get the opportunity to learn new skills, but they also get to know themselves and become lifelong learners.

Rose says, "Personalized learning platforms like Degreed help people know themselves—I mean really, really know who they are. Sure, people are there to learn something, but personalized learning helps you to absolutely understand yourself as an individual. You're developing incredible skills to be a lifelong learner and to know what you're expert at, and to look at the things you are learning and connect that to real life. We need to support that journey."[18]

How to Embrace Personalized Learning

Once you have decided that you want your employees to have a personalized learning experience, how do you get started? Below are some ways that you can begin the personalized learning journey at your company.

1. Help people understand their skills, strengths, and weaknesses

Assessments are a great way to help employees and managers understand each employee's skills, strengths, and weaknesses. There are so many different types of assessments in the market, and the ones you choose depend on how in-depth you want to go with the personalization. Many companies and leaders are familiar with 360 assessments where an employee does a self-assessment and receives feedback from their manager and peers. There are also free, online assessments for individuals. Pluralsight, for example, empowers developers to take a simple knowledge check to measure the extent of their programming skills, which in turn enables them to personalize their learning. Degreed also provides a method of identifying the skills you have versus the skills you need (more about that in chapter 8). The main goal is to give employees a personalized view of themselves so that their learning and skill plans can be tailored for them. It's smart to keep it simple though— think about how many skills you can realistically work on in a given year.

2. Create personalized learning plans

Once employees have a good sense of what skills they want to focus on, they can create a personalized learning or skill plan based on self-knowledge and their learning and career goals. It's motivating for employees to know what they need to focus on and to chart their progress toward their goals. This is different from a development plan that is part of a performance review, which almost seems punitive. Instead, learning plans are a good way to create an inspiring career vision that will motivate your employees to want to learn new skills.

3. Create flexible, supportive learning environments

As soon as your employees have a good sense of the types of skills they want to focus on, it is up to leaders and managers to guide their learning. But more importantly, it's crucial to provide an environment where they feel safe to both fail and succeed when taking on their new challenges. This means encouraging your employees to learn on the job and giving people the time they need to develop the skills they've identified. Also, if you know what skills your employees are trying to build, you can give them assignments that will stretch and challenge them personally and professionally. It may not always be comfortable for your employees, especially overachievers, to jump into areas where they don't feel completely competent, but with support and encouragement, these opportunities can help shape a career.

CHAPTER FOUR

Combat Content Overload

W HEN YOU WANT to learn something, what's the first thing you do? You might turn to Google, but depending on what you're looking for, the answers may not be as simple as you think. For example, say you want to know more about social media. If you Google "social media," you are faced with over 250 million search results. If you try to be more specific and type in "learning social media" instead, the results narrow to about 30 million, which is better, but let's face it, still overwhelming. The problem is that we simply can't keep up with the amount of information that's being created in the world.

Most experts predict that the size of the digital universe is at least doubling every two years (based on a 50-fold growth from 2010 to 2020).[1] As a consequence of this content overload, we have become overwhelmed by the constant surge of information, impatient in our need for information "right now," and distracted by the never-ending stream of websites, apps, and video clips. We spend so much time trying to sift through information that only a fraction of a typical working week is left over for learning.

Yet it is not all bad news. There are ways we can learn to combat content overload if we choose the right learning tools. In this chapter, we'll talk about different types of learning content and how real companies are putting them to use to help their employees learn, gain expertise, and build skills.

The Moment of Need

While the sheer volume of information out there may prove overwhelming, there are ways for us to learn what we want and build our own learning journey. Think about the rich diversity of sources we can learn from throughout our lives. Excellent learning content is everywhere. Never have we had the opportunity to learn about any topic, from any device, anywhere in the world at such a low or even no cost. And this is only the beginning of the democratization of content, where people have immediate access to the information they need. All this information at our fingertips is a good thing, but only if we can help overwhelmed learners find what they need, the moment they need it.

That moment of need usually happens on the job. For example, say you need to figure out how to use data to tell a compelling story and present it to your boss the next day. You can't wait for a class on "Telling your Story with Data." You need the information now. How great would it be if you could easily find what you want without wading through millions of search results?

Interestingly, when we are in our moment of need, Google isn't the first resource that we turn to. A research study carried out by Degreed in 2016[2] found that when people want to learn something, they first ask their peers, bosses, or mentors before searching the internet. The last thing they do is consult their HR department or learning organization. The results show that people like to learn from each other as well as from technology. Companies should take notice of these results, and leaders should ask themselves, "When I want to learn something, how do I learn?" It is only by truly understanding how each of us learns that we will be able to build a learning platform that works for each and every employee.

Tim Quinlan, director of digital platforms for Intel,[3] understood the importance of individual learning when he was putting together his digital learning strategy for the company. When the time came to present his strategy to his boss, he didn't use PowerPoint presentations or spreadsheets to show the value of learning. He simply talked to his boss and asked him how he liked to learn. His boss explained that he often searched for information online but couldn't always find what he was looking for. So, Quinlan asked him to do the same search on Degreed, his proposed learning technology platform. His boss was both surprised and pleased to find what he wanted right away in the form of curated content and learning pathways. As Quinlan demonstrated, the ability to aggregate learning assets and to curate learning content to help employees discover what they need, when they need it, is the first step to building new knowledge and skills.

Consumerization of Content

When combating content overload and helping overwhelmed employees, it's good to first understand just what types of online learning resources are available and how companies are using them. There is some debate about what constitutes learning content. It used to be that companies provided training in two forms: either by instructor-led classroom training or through e-learning. Learning organizations would either create all of their own learning content or hire expensive vendors to create custom content for them. Kelly recalls that one IT department spent more than $300,000 for a vendor to create a single online compliance course for its employees!

For decades, online learning often conjured up images of boring PowerPoint presentations with voiceovers, or some sort of awful compliance training. But today, there are hundreds of companies using thoughtful and innovative learning content on just about any topic imaginable. Some learning content comes in the form of content libraries that individuals or companies can pay for through a subscription service; other content is free and can be accessed by anyone. Even online compliance training can be entertaining thanks to companies like Second City,[4] the comedy troupe, who have contributed to making them not just relevant, but also fun and engaging.

The real benefit to online learning is that new content is being created every day, sharing information on the latest technologies, the latest methodologies, and the most up-to-date research, enabling us to access this information as it becomes available—sometimes instantly. Yet not all of us know about it, even those who consider themselves to be lifelong learners. When the Pew Research Center did a survey of lifelong learning and technology in 2016,[5] it found that, while over 70 percent of American adults surveyed considered themselves lifelong learners, and over 50 percent of full- or part-time workers took part in work or career learning, the majority of adults had little to no awareness of the technology and resources available to them. Here is the breakdown:

- 61 percent little or no awareness of distance learning
- 79 percent little or no awareness of Khan Academy (video lessons)
- 80 percent little or no awareness of Massive Open Online Courses (MOOCs)
- 83 percent little or no awareness of digital badges

Digital learning content is rapidly evolving, so it is important to understand what content is available, what's working, and where companies and employees are being successful. Building awareness of these valuable resources is an important step toward improving the quality of learning in organizations. Low- and no-cost quality digital content is now so widely available that organizations simply cannot afford to overlook the learning content available.

Choosing the best content for employees has never been easier. For example, the free online video platform TED (Technology, Education, and Design) provides access to a collection of short (18 minutes or less), impactful talks from thought leaders around the world. Bill Gates (Microsoft), Elon Musk (Tesla), Jeff Bezos (Amazon), Sergey Brin (Google), and Steve Jobs (Apple) are just a few business leaders who have given inspirational talks on TED. In addition, lesser-known thought leaders speak on topics ranging from Garry Kasparov on artificial intelligence to Brené Brown on the power of vulnerability. Many companies use the videos as part of their learning content offerings to help employees think more creatively and inspire innovation and purpose at work.

YouTube is another popular information source and offers a variety of instructional videos, unparalleled by any other media. For example,

David has used YouTube to learn everything from how to change a tire on his bicycle to concepts about data science and neuroscience for work. Millions of people post "how-to" videos on YouTube regularly. Some of the most popular educational and instructional videos on YouTube are posted by Khan Academy.

Khan Academy

The birth of Khan Academy is a well-known story in the education world. It started over a decade ago when educator Sal Khan's cousin, Nadia, asked him for some tutoring in math and science because she was falling way behind in her class at school. Because Khan lived in Boston and Nadia lived in New Orleans, he would tutor her by phone. His method helped Nadia excel; in fact, she went from practically failing math to becoming the top student in her class. Because of these great results, more and more of Khan's extended family asked him for personal tutoring too. And so it went until one of his friends suggested that he make videos of the lessons and make them available online, so they could all view the lessons at their convenience and make the whole process more efficient.

Over time, Khan made hundreds then thousands of learning videos and posted them on YouTube, and although Khan was not the first person to post online educational videos, something about his style attracted a huge audience. For some across the world without access to education, it changed their lives.

When Khan Academy became more well-known and even when it went beyond being a hobby, Khan said that the content was crafted from a more personal point of view. It started with some math he knew and then some science, but then he started getting into anatomy and certain subjects he didn't know as well. Learning about other subjects made it fun for Khan. And it continues to be fun for Khan: "I spend about 30 to 40 percent of my time continuing to make content, and I consider that the best part of my job. I consider myself the luckiest person because it's what I like. I don't know any other job where you can spend 30 to 40 percent of your time learning new things—and use that knowledge to help others."[6]

As his audience grew, Khan became passionate about providing learning to those who otherwise might not ever receive any education. He attracted some big investors like the Skoll Foundation, the Bill & Melinda Gates Foundation, and Google, who all saw his offering as a real catalyst for change in the world of education. More than 10 years later, the Khan Academy, which is a nonprofit, has delivered more than one billion lessons online. The content is all free and is used by eight million learners monthly around the world.[7] It has evolved to include lessons on math, science, arts, humanities, economics, and test preparation, to name a few. Overall, Khan has succeeded in revolutionizing education in a way that has drastically changed the way we learn and absorb new content.

The "Flipped Classroom"

What Khan has done has extended far beyond student education and learning. His approach has influenced corporate learning in a big way. His videos have enabled some teachers to "flip" their classroom[8] where students are instructed to watch video lectures on their own then use class time for discussion and guidance. This concept has challenged what corporate learning could and should be.

Some companies have already applied the flipped classroom to corporate learning. Through this model, employees derive the "knowledge" part of learning in their own time, at their own pace, by watching a video (like Khan's cousin Nadia did). Companies then bring those employees together, in person, and use that valuable time to interact with peers, practice skills, and solve real business problems. The combination of online learning content and in-person meetings is a powerful force for learning and collaboration. In the corporate world, taking time away from work to attend training is extremely expensive and inefficient (think of how much money companies spend on classes, hotels, and plane tickets, not to mention the cost of employees being away from their jobs).

As a leader, if you are going to bring people together, you need to make it count. That means using the time for employees to learn from peers, have meaningful discussions about the content and concepts they have learned, and create solutions to pressing problems. This is just one way to help companies achieve success.

Khan Academy Goes Corporate

The Khan Academy recently started to partner with companies to help their employees and their customers build skills. For example, they partnered with Bank of America to create a program for their customers on financial acumen called BetterMoneyHabits.com,[9] and then followed that with a program to help new college grads figure out careers and personal finance. The latter features videos that help young adults think about their careers and weigh their passion against the financial implications of any given career.

The videos Khan Academy produces feature young professionals talking about what it's like to have a particular career, what skills they need, and how much money they make, which offers a glimpse of what life in the working world is like. Helping new college graduates understand what's available for them in a job and a career is something that we should spend more time on given that, according to Accenture,[10] eight out of 10 new college grads do not have a job lined up at graduation. According to Bank of America research, 60 percent of new college grads place more importance on passion than on their paycheck, but they need to understand the financial realities of that choice as well.

The Khan Academy was not the only learning resource to break new ground. About the same time, a new learning content resource was on the horizon that would further advance the democratization of education on a global level.

Massive Open Online Courses (MOOCs)

In 2011, something unprecedented occurred: two Stanford University professors launched three online courses (MOOCs) that allowed free access to the same learning content that was made available to Stanford students.

This was a big deal, especially because Stanford University is known as one of the most difficult and prestigious universities in the world, where a mere 4.8 percent of 44,000 applicants were accepted in 2016.[11]

Essentially, it was an experiment to offer self-paced, scalable, accessible, and affordable online learning to anyone, anywhere in the world. When the first Stanford MOOC, *Introduction to Artificial Intelligence*, was launched, 160,000 students around the world signed up.[12]

MOOCs offer learners access to online lectures and assign homework that is graded by a computer. When the class and coursework have been completed, participants receive a certificate of accomplishment. MOOCs are really the next evolution of the distance-learning model where people learn remotely without having to physically be in a classroom. Two companies were formed because of the first three MOOCs that were offered from Stanford: Coursera and Udacity. The most well-known nonprofit MOOC provider is EdX. During the past three years, over 25 million people from around the world have enrolled, and while completion rates are low (around 4 percent for Coursera) the overall reach is still significant.[13]

While the original goal for MOOCs was to make education more accessible to those who wouldn't otherwise be able to afford it, studies during the past five years have shown some interesting trends. According to *Harvard Business Review*, "Enrollees predominantly are well-educated residents of developed countries," and many people are using MOOCS to build skills and advance their careers. "Fifty-two percent of the people surveyed report a primary goal of improving their current job or finding a new job—they are 'career builders.' Of these career builders, 87 percent report a career benefit of some kind."[14]

Since Coursera and Udacity were founded, they have evolved their business models to focus on learning for working professionals rather than just undergraduate students. They connect a company and/or a university together and create learning content focused on a particular topic. For example, Udacity partnered with Mercedes-Benz to create a project-based program on self-driving cars, while Coursera partnered with Google to create a course on big data and machine learning using the Google Cloud.[15]

This collaboration between industry and education benefits people who potentially want to work for the company that's sponsoring the learning or break into a new career. For example, say you want to be a self-driving car engineer for Mercedes-Benz. Taking the course created by Udacity gives you an advantage in the recruiting process. This also benefits the company (in this case Mercedes-Benz) since they will attract applicants who already know how to use their products (their new self-driving car). The fact that companies are now realizing they need to get involved in helping build skills for the future is a positive sign, particularly since universities have been struggling to keep up with the rapidly changing landscape of new jobs and skills.

AXA, the largest insurance company in France, realizes the importance of providing relevant content to their employees to prepare them for the jobs of the future.[16] The organization recently announced a global partnership with Coursera to help foster a self-directed learning model that provides relevant skills to a subset of their employees. One thousand employees will have access to a library of Coursera offerings to upskill in business acumen. Fifty percent of the cohort will get certifications, and AXA employees in 64 countries will gain access to more than 300 courses in topics such as leadership, digital marketing, and data science. L'Oréal is another global company using Coursera to help their employees build skills. The company targets 50 percent of their employees' learning through self-directed or digital initiatives.[17]

Still, many companies seem to be missing a big part of how they can be more competitive in hiring and retaining great talent. According to Monika Hamori in *Harvard Business Review*, "A lot of people who want to become better at their jobs are fending for themselves."[18] Companies are reluctant to invest in talent that may end up leaving to work for the competition. On the flipside, employees see further learning as an investment in themselves and their future. One of the reasons many companies don't support their employees' learning through MOOCs is because they lack awareness of the impact MOOCs have, such as low course fees, no travel costs, and less disruption to day-to-day work. If we could bring companies and employees together around how they engage in MOOCs, it would be a huge win-win situation.

Learning Content Libraries

When it comes to online learning content, video tutorials and MOOCs are only the tip of the iceberg. There are hundreds of subscription-based, paid online learning libraries on the market today. Some of the most popular include OpenSesame, Pluralsight, Safari, Lynda.com, Skillsoft, Creative Live, Treehouse, and Udemy. Content libraries provide hundreds if not thousands of courses and/or video content to help employees learn about topics at their own pace asynchronously. Some content libraries are vast and cover a wide variety of topics and skills, while others specialize in areas like technology. Individuals can buy subscriptions so they can learn on their own time, and many companies buy companywide subscriptions to provide access for all their employees.

Utah-based Pluralsight provides a content library of learning videos focused on the technology sector. The technical learning content created by experts in the field is video based and helps people build skills in mobile development, web development, machine learning, artificial intelligence, and virtual reality, to name a few. In addition to the learning content, participants are also offered skill assessments, learning checks, and discussion boards.

Recently, Google partnered with Pluralsight as part of an initiative to tackle India's skills gap challenge.[19] According to NASSCOM, India's IT training association, the Google/Pluralsight partnership is helping 3.9 million people in India update the technology skills they need to stay relevant in the workplace. In addition, the partnership is focused on helping skill new developers for the 150,000 new tech jobs that are coming online within the year.

Microlearning

Microlearning is the opposite of typical corporate training; instead of sitting for eight hours in a classroom, microlearning serves bite-sized learning content, usually lasting only a few minutes and easily accessible by mobile phone. New York City–based technology company Grovo is most well-known for microlearning. According to the Association for Talent Development, 92 percent of organizations currently using microlearning plan to do more of it, while the 67 percent of organizations not using it plan to start using it.[20]

Companies adopt microlearning content because it seems to work. First, people can fit short bursts of learning into their work routine without having to take time out to go to a training class. Microlearning also helps people to get just enough content to help them with the task at hand. Finally, microlearning is useful for reinforcing learning and helping people recall content and concepts. A number of companies have embraced microlearning, including Gap, Chevron, and PepsiCo.[21]

According to Maksim Ovsyannikov, former vice president of product for Grovo, microlearning was developed so that content could be more concise and with specific takeaways. In about five minutes or less, a typical piece of microlearning content attempts to:

- State a problem
- Summarize why it is important
- Propose a solution
- Give an example of how this solution can be applied
- Summarize and quiz

Ovsyannikov gives this example: "Imagine a new manager who is about to conduct her first one-on-one. An insightful microlearning lesson can give her valuable information on effective one-on-ones quickly and in the moment of need, right before she is about to walk into this type of first interaction."[22]

According to Ovsyannikov, there are two great misconceptions with microlearning. "First is the misconception that it is not possible to deliver broader areas of knowledge via microlearning, and that microlearning can only be used to microlearn."[23]

That is not accurate. Microlearning can be effectively combined into learning pathways where bits of knowledge are delivered daily over a period of time. As such, the learner can acquire a skill that is not tied to one piece of microlearning, but instead is gained through a series of microlearning lessons delivered in the same path.

The second major misconception with microlearning exists among the content providers, some of whom promote the message that if the content doesn't come from them, then it doesn't count as microlearning. This is an inaccurate interpretation given that microlearning can be developed by anyone who follows sound instructional design principles. This involves simply shortening the content to make it more concise, while constantly testing and summarizing the knowledge being delivered.

Ovsyannikov goes on to say, "Almost anyone can build microlearning; in fact, it is easier to build microlearning content than traditional learning content because it is more agile and more iterative."[24]

Curated Content

With all the different types of learning content available, the big question becomes: How do companies and employees figure out what to choose? Curating content is a great strategy for helping employees find what they need just when they need it. Let's take an example. Say you want to learn more about cybersecurity. You could try googling it, but you have a colleague, Julie, who works in the engineering group at your company, and she is a subject matter expert on this topic. You ask Julie what she thinks are the best learning resources surrounding cybersecurity. In response, Julie puts together a list of courses, conferences, certificates, books, podcasts, websites, experiences, journals, and articles that she thinks are the most valuable sources of information.

Now imagine that you have technology that will let you put these resources in a guided digital pathway so that anyone who wants to learn about cybersecurity can also see the list of resources that Julie put together. That's curated content. Instead of employees guessing which resources are the best, they learn from someone who is an expert already.

The great thing about curated content pathways is that they open learning in a whole new way. Not only can learning professionals in the corporate learning organization curate content on various topics, but also employees who are already subject matter experts are able to share their expertise. This means that all employees can get involved in learning and teaching others. Empowering employees to choose pathways of learning that make sense to them is a powerful way to close the skills gap and build on their expertise.

MasterCard has been using the power of curating content for several years. The company came up with a creative way to encourage all employees to share their expertise. They held a contest where they challenged employees to identify a topic they were passionate about, and then create their own pathways of curated content to teach other employees about the topic. When all the submissions were in, the top three pathways were chosen, and the curators were awarded prizes for their efforts. It was fun and competitive, but most importantly, it got everyone engaged in the learning process and created exceptional resources for the benefit of all of their employees.

Curating Content Using Machine Learning

Imagine a scenario where every employee in the world has access to personalized learning, and that learning helps them build the knowledge and skills they need throughout their careers. Just a few short years ago, the idea that one day everyone could have access to the learning they needed when they needed it seemed like a fantasy. Now, with the rise of machine learning, it's entirely possible for anyone to have a personalized learning experience. Now you can have relevant learning content served to you and your employees every day based on your interests, on who you are, on what you do, on how you like to learn, on what skills you want to build, and on who you know. Think about what this means.

That was the dream, but it's gradually becoming a reality through machine learning. Machine learning is a subset of artificial intelligence (AI), and it gives computers the ability to learn from data without being explicitly programmed. In other words, the computer learns how to learn. So what role does machine learning play in corporate education? Its uses are twofold. First, it helps personalize the employee's learning experience by learning the type of content being consumed by that user and second, it codifies the skills and knowledge being gained from this content.

Machine learning organizes and recommends learning based on your interests. Think of what Spotify has done for music or Netflix for movies. The more you watch or listen, the more the technology learns about you. The more it learns about you, the better it is at giving you more of what you want, or might want. This allows you to discover new music based on your preferences (in the form of customized playlists) and inspires ideas about what movies you might want to watch next (through suggestions and recommendations).

"Machine learning is not just about content recommendations," says James Densmore, director of data science at Degreed. "I get a lot of feedback from people thinking that machine learning is about building better recommendation systems, when in fact the ultimate goal is to understand why we are recommending a given piece of content. Is it the format (course versus article), the length, the frequency of consumption, the author, or something else?"[25]

IBM's supercomputer Watson illustrates nicely how machine learning works. Watson was famously able to beat humans at the quiz show *Jeopardy* because of its ability to process thousands of questions and learn how to play the game. Machine learning is at the heart of so much of the technology we use today, yet we're not that aware of it because it's working in the background. Many of the biggest technology firms use machine learning for many of our day-to-day tasks. For example, Amazon recommends products on every page; Google shows you ads that it thinks are relevant to you (and sometimes asks you if they are right, thus getting more data); and Facebook uses face recognition to identify people in pictures you post.

When you apply this to learning technology, as we are doing at Degreed, machine learning allows learning to be curated automatically. It gives you a selection of learning content that is personalized and relevant. You can receive a feed of new learning content to consider on a daily basis, and learning pathways are recommended to you based on what you want to learn and what the system is learning about you. It does the processing so you don't have to wade through thousands of pieces of content. You can focus on learning. It then enables you to analyze the data so that you understand what skills your employees are building.

Think about how efficient this process is in comparison with the typical "needs analysis"—the manual process used by many learning professionals to ascertain employees' knowledge, skills, and abilities. While regular needs analyses can provide useful information when it comes to designing new content or programs, it is time consuming and rarely meets the needs and demands of the employees taking part.

With machine learning in corporate education, we can collect and analyze the data to truly understand what employees are learning. The data can tell you what content your employees are consuming, which content and modalities they prefer, and most importantly, what skills they are building. There has never been a better way to get insights about your learners—not what your employees say they want to learn, but what they are learning.

Creating a Digital Learning Strategy

Many companies are rethinking their learning strategy with a view to incorporating more digital components to create a culture that encourages continuous learning. In her book *Stretch: How to Future-Proof Yourself for Tomorrow's Workplace,* Karie Willyerd[26] discusses how to stay current in the workforce. She says, "It's not that you have to drop everything you are doing and go reskill yourself. It's more that it's important to keep learning all the time." She likens learning to staying in shape physically, in that it's better to exercise moderately over the course of your life rather than try to run a marathon and then quit.

Willyerd says, "Individuals and companies need to set up platforms and ways for people to be constantly learning to set a culture and tone and expectation around continuous learning. That's probably the only way that you can keep up. It's counterproductive not to pay attention to this, and then go through a major restructuring and hire all new people only to have them become obsolete as well."

Ask yourself how you learn every day. Do you search for content on Google and watch videos online? Most people, including your employees, learn from a variety of informal sources. So, when you are creating your digital learning strategy to incorporate digital learning assets into your offering, think about the following questions to help you develop your plan.

1. What is a digital learning strategy?

A digital learning strategy is the process of incorporating digital learning assets (videos, online learning, courses, blogs, articles, and books) to help people learn. But, digital learning is more than that—it encourages us to think about learning in a different way. There is so much content for learning available to people now, and the rate of change is so fast, that we can't be bound by old models of learning (like classroom training) to satisfy the required skills today.

A digital learning strategy provides us with the opportunity to direct people to digital assets we have developed, or that already exist, and make that content more on-demand. Having a variety of digital asset types also considers all the different ways people like to learn: Kelly loves to read books or listen to podcasts to learn; David prefers to watch videos and read articles; and others may like to take a multiweek online course. So, it is a good idea to build a plan into the digital learning strategy for how these digital learning assets should be offered to employees.

2. Why do organizations need a digital learning strategy?

One reason it's so valuable to have a digital learning strategy is that it provides learning to all employees—not just the chosen few. It also enables companies to react more nimbly to shifting priorities as well as specialized learning needs that can't always be accommodated with the resources available.

When a digital learning strategy is deployed, it instantly becomes a global, scalable benefit for all employees, proving to them that the company is investing in them and their skill development—all the time. Instead of employees having to go through the learning department to develop a particular type of learning, they have thousands of learning assets at their fingertips whenever they need them.

Many companies spend most of their learning budgets on leaders, managers, or high-performing employees, and then leave the rest of their employees to fend for themselves. Having a digital strategy helps reach all employees, and it provides the company with a competitive advantage: employees are more likely to stay in a company that invests in skill building and further learning.

3. What type of digital content should be included?

Here's where a little analysis and iteration comes into play. When Kelly was at LinkedIn, she and her team were trying to decide which content to include in the digital strategy. LinkedIn was just starting the learning organization, so the team hadn't created content yet. To get learning content to people quickly, the team partnered with a few leading content providers that had libraries of digital content.

Kelly and her team chose three of those content partners. During the first year they tracked the usage of this partner content to see what employees were using to learn. They also included some of the free content, such as TED Talks and YouTube videos. That worked well for creating the first digital strategy. But over time, as LinkedIn learned what was working best for its employees, the company dropped some partner content and added some company-specific digital content to the mix.

4. How do organizations know what their employees are learning online?

The key to finding out the impact of the first digital learning strategy is to try to obtain data on what employees are consuming and learning, and then to use that information to refine the strategy. However, it can be time consuming to track and understand what people are learning through such a range of informal learning assets (videos, blogs, and books). Traditional technologies such as LMS are able to track something people registered for (like an event or class), but they are unable to track informal learning and activities.

While it is possible to manually track informal learning, it is a very arduous process. It is even more difficult to get to a personalized view of each employee's learning. New technologies like Degreed have solved the personalized analytics problem by providing a detailed view of how people engage with digital learning content, much like fitness trackers have automated gathering personal fitness records.

How to Help Overwhelmed Learners

In this chapter, we've talked about the sheer amount of content that is available for learning. We've also talked about the different types of content, how companies are using them, and how you can create a digital learning strategy. There's no doubt that we are all overwhelmed by the amount of learning content out there. Below are some ways you can help overwhelmed learners at your company.

1. Curate content

There are a few ways you can curate content. However, there is a huge distinction between curated content and aggregated content. An example of aggregated content is when you do a Google search on a topic such as "social media" and you get hundreds, if not thousands, of search results. You still have to sort through all the results and decide about what is most *relevant* to you, and that takes a lot of time. Curated content, on the other hand, is a way to give an employee only the best and most relevant pieces of content for that subject area. It means narrowing down the choices so that people are not so overwhelmed. There are a few different ways to provide curated content.

Curated pathways of content

One way to curate content is to provide a "pathway" of learning. This means that instead of just choosing one learning asset among a few, you create a collection of assets that can either be consumed in order (or not) depending on the goal.

For example, you have seven learning assets in the collection. You might get a video to introduce the subject, then a portion of a class or book, a podcast, two articles, and even an assessment to see how well you've comprehended the topic area. This "pathway" can be incredibly useful for prescriptive learning for topic areas such as sales training or management development, but it can also be very helpful for onboarding new employees to a company or into their functional groups (sales, engineering, and marketing).

The flexibility of learning pathways is also a plus in that you can use pathways created by others, modify existing pathways to make them more relevant for your audience, or create a completely new pathway.

Social curation

The idea that learners like to learn from both peers and experts is nothing new, but social curation makes this learning come to life. Imagine that you are an engineer at a company and you are trying to learn about the latest technology. Then you find curated content from an expert or a peer who already knows much more about this technology than you do. Instantly you have content from a reliable source that is relevant to what you need to learn. And, with social curation, you can not only consume this content, you can add your own, rate it, or recommend it to others. This is the power of social curation.

Machine-curated content

Some learning platforms use machine learning to understand what content you are most interested in and what content is most relevant to you. For example, if you are interested in learning how to get better at giving presentations, the learning platform can then serve up five relevant pieces of content to you per day based on what it knows about you. If you consume the content, it gives you more of that kind of content, but if you dismiss it, it tries to find more relevant content for you. The more you use it, the more it learns about what you like and what's most relevant to you.

2. Recommend content

Another great way to help the overwhelmed learner is to make recommendations about relevant content. For example, a manager could easily share existing content that they think would be incredibly useful to their team by simply recommending it. They can do this through an integrated learning platform that will easily track what content they recommend, and how and when people consume that content. The platform will capture team discussions around that content.

3. Do not create new content

When thinking about creating content, many people naturally jump to creating something new and original. In some cases, that may be the best approach, but given what we know about the overwhelmed learner, creating new content may not be necessary.

When Kelly attended an offsite for a tech company, which brought together a large number of learning leaders to coordinate their content strategy, they soon discovered that there were 15 different, but similar, courses on the same topic—in this case the topic was project management. This happened because people didn't have a view into all the content that was out there (even in one company, let alone across the internet). Many different people had created content that lived in content management systems, web servers, learning management systems, on wikis, and on people's computers. This is not a unique problem for companies. Having an integrated learning platform helps solve this problem.

When you think about creating content, find out if that content already exists either at your company or free on the internet. If you do this, you can then spend time creating content that is specific to your company or your expertise rather than duplicating content that is already high quality and serves the purpose.

4. Encourage employees to set learning goals

When employees set goals around their learning, they focus on what they should be spending their time on. For example, say Jenn wants to focus on learning more about business strategy. She could set a learning goal to outline how she might acquire this skill (books, podcasts, classes, mentoring, etc.). Then she could track her progress against her goal and even gain certification for that skill upon completion.

5. Let employees own their career development

Instead of mandating training from the top down, many companies encourage employees to own and direct their own learning and career development. Willyerd says that one of the overarching imperatives to understand is, "It's all on you! There is no magic person behind the curtain who is thinking about your career and planning for it and making sure that you get everything you need, whether it's the learning that you need or the experiences that you need."

Willyerd goes on to say, "A manager is incented to put whoever is best or most productive onto a project, so if you don't speak up and look for the experiences or learning you need, you will miss out."[27]

While organizations can put together tools, processes, and guidelines to help people develop, it's up to the employee to do what it takes to get what they need. In other words, employees need to take advantage of all the content that is available and understand that while managers may guide them, they are the ones in the driver's seat.

CHAPTER FIVE

Understand the Power of Peers

I N 2006, KELLY decided to go back to school to study learning and education technology in parallel with her full-time role as senior director of learning products in Silicon Valley. It had been many years since she received any formal education and school had changed much more than she had realized.

Instead of sitting in huge lecture halls filled with hundreds of anonymous students feverishly taking notes, she found herself in a social environment collaborating with her peers. The lone professor lecturing at the front of the room had been largely replaced by virtual classes equipped with online collaborative learning tools. Students would watch video lectures and would then be asked questions about what they had learned.

This new environment of peer-to-peer learning created a safe space for each student to share information, viewpoints, and experience. It was a place where even the most introverted students felt compelled to speak up, a space where everyone had a voice.

But it didn't stop there. The students would then share their thoughts on the responses given by their peers. Kelly found herself engaging with her peers, learning about others' ideas, experiences, and opinions. As the program went on, Kelly realized that she was learning as much if not more from her peers than she had learned from her college professors all those years earlier.

It prompted Kelly to start asking herself questions: What if employees could develop their expertise by tapping into their desire to learn from and collaborate with their peers? What if learning was integrated into work, and collaboration with coworkers was the prominent form of learning in the workplace? This new learning experience convinced Kelly of the power of peer-to-peer learning for organizations.

Why Learning Cannot Be "Ordered Up" Like Fast Food

In the corporate world, "peers" may or may not be in the same work group. Unlike the traditional expert-to-student learning where one person tends to outrank another in terms of responsibilities or position, peer learning begins on a level playing field where everybody feels comfortable to engage and collaborate with each other either in person or online.

Typically, in peer-to-peer learning there will be someone *facilitating* the learning process. Learning facilitators make sure everyone stays on topic, notes key ideas and themes, and keeps the conversation moving forward. The rest of the participants must be prepared to go "all-in" by openly communicating with the group, actively giving and receiving feedback, and helping others learn, where possible. Of course, successful peer-to-peer learning only comes about when organizations implement it, which, as Kelly found out, isn't all that often.

It has been more than 10 years since Kelly studied learning and education technology in a master's program, yet when it comes to corporate learning in organizations, things have been slow to evolve. Most organizations still depend on outdated learning management systems, training courses delivered through PowerPoint presentations by someone in HR, or outsourced vendor programs. Over $130 billion is spent this way on corporate training in the US, with organizations struggling to see the benefits.[1]

One problem is that many managers and leaders tend to see learning as something that you do once, check the box, and you are done. Want to make employees more culturally aware? Send them on a diversity training program. Managers not hiring the right people? Put them in front of a PowerPoint presentation and get someone to lecture them on interviewing skills. Research shows that the people taking part in these programs either resent being there in the first place or simply forget what they've been taught within the space of a couple of days or even hours.[2]

The point is that learning cannot be ordered up like a burger in a fast-food restaurant. There is no quick fix. Learning is about gaining new skills and knowledge from the people around us; in fact, studies have shown that even the act of learning itself is a major contributor to job satisfaction.[3]

Closing the Generation Gap

These days, most companies have a workforce made up of four generations. Millennials work alongside baby boomers and gen-Xers, and now gen-Zers are starting to enter the workforce. Sometimes generational differences can get in the way of working together in harmony. Peer-to-peer learning is a valuable way of uniting a multigenerational workforce because it enables people to teach each other on a level playing field. When people are in an environment that allows them to listen to different perspectives and share their own knowledge and expertise, they gradually develop a greater understanding of each other.

But it's more than just sharing knowledge. Peer-to-peer learning creates a workplace environment that actually raises the bar on what is expected. According to a study in Germany analyzing millions of workers over a 15-year span, healthy social pressure pushes people to do better: "When an employee is around other high performers, they feel pressure to keep up with their colleagues, which leads to an environment where coworkers themselves raise the bar on what is expected."[4]

The study showed, however, that performance tends to dip when top performers exit the team, leading to the suggestion that "when top performers leave, their positive impact leaves too."

Social learning theory says that we learn best by observing someone else's behavior and then imitating it. Psychologist Albert Bandura writes, "Most human behavior is learned observationally through modeling: from observing others, one forms an idea of how new behaviors are performed, and on later occasions this coded information serves as a guide for action."[5]

In fact, there is a different dynamic altogether in learning from our peers versus learning from someone in a superior position. Regardless of the relationship you may have with your boss, the reality is that when you work for someone, they ultimately have power over you—the power to help you with your career, to mentor you and champion your efforts, to impact your income and your yearly bonuses, and to promote you or fire you. These factors often inhibit us from saying what we want to say or speaking up when there is a concern.

The other dynamic to peer learning is reciprocity. People receive feedback from the group for their own work, and they tend to put more time and energy into providing meaningful feedback on their peers' work as well. That simply doesn't happen when the boss is delivering one-way feedback to employees.

Peer-to-peer learning is a vital part of the learning journey, but why do so few organizations implement it? Jaime Casap, education evangelist at Google, believes that peer-to-peer learning does not come naturally to us.

> *The problem is we're not open to peer-to-peer learning as a society. And what I mean by that is we talk about collaboration in education, but we don't mean it. We teach kids to be individuals and to value individual accomplishments.*[6]

In other words, the idea of sharing knowledge and exchanging honest feedback with our peers goes against traditional learning, where the focus is more on assessing people singularly. However, the peer-to-peer learning process can switch that focus and provide us with a whole new set of skills.

The Peer-to-Peer Learning Process

As we learned in chapter 1, there are four steps to the learning process, which we call "the Learning Loop." The steps are obtaining knowledge, practicing what we have learned, and getting feedback, followed by reflecting on the whole learning experience.

Peer-to-peer learning provides us with deeper levels of learning by going through the entire learning loop.

- Gain knowledge
- Practice by applying the knowledge
- Get feedback
- Reflect on what has been learned

Take Priya, for instance. When Priya was trying out a new role in product management, she reached out to other product managers in the company to gain knowledge by understanding their roles better. When it came to actually produce the product plan, she asked for sample product plans from other product managers so she could practice what "good" looks like for this group and this company. Once Priya put together her first product plan, she asked the other product managers for feedback. After she received feedback, she took some time to reflect on what she had learned throughout the process.

By completing the peer-to-peer learning process and going through all the phases of the learning cycle, we gain other valuable skills, including self-reflection, critical thinking, and how to effectively give and receive feedback.

Self-reflection skills

Self-reflection is the ability to ultimately know yourself or be willing to get to know yourself better. Being able to self-reflect can also positively impact our work performance. A study focused on call centers shows that people who spent 15 minutes at the end of each day over the course of 10 days reflecting on what they had learned performed their work 23 percent better than those who did not self-reflect.[7]

When self-reflection is applied to learning, especially in the context of "learning how to learn" or in demonstrating learning agility, it provides the foundation for understanding our own strengths and weaknesses, keeping an open mind, accepting constructive criticism, and applying those insights to something more productive. One of the many benefits of peer-to-peer learning is that it gives us the opportunity to reflect on our own work. It also gives us space to think more deeply about the work of others to provide thoughtful feedback. As management expert Peter Drucker once said, "Follow effective action with quiet reflection. From the quiet reflection will come even more effective action."[8]

Critical-thinking skills

Next, the peer-to-peer learning process helps improve our critical thinking skills. Critical thinking is the ability to use our knowledge and intellect to analyze information or situations without judgment or bias to make balanced, thoughtful, evidence-based decisions and resolutions.

During the past 10 years, critical thinking has become one of the most highly sought traits in employees, and it is still an important skill for the future. A recent report called "The Future of Jobs" by the World Economic Forum shows that critical-thinking skills will rise in demand as organizations rush to deal with an ever-increasing variety of complex problems.[9]

Giving and receiving constructive feedback

Finally, peer-to-peer learning helps us master the difficult skills of giving and accepting constructive feedback. Giving honest feedback, listening, and being able to receive feedback may be some of the most important skills of all. Most people are better at giving positive feedback because it makes everyone involved feel good, including the giver. Yet most people shy away from giving negative or constructive feedback because they do not want to hurt or disappoint people. Let's face it, sometimes it's much easier not to say anything at all. However, successful peer-to-peer learning gives people the confidence to provide constructive feedback and receive it without a feeling of defensiveness.

In an ideal world, everyone would successfully learn something of value, and then focus on self-reflection, critical thinking, and providing and accepting thoughtful feedback. In the corporate world it is rare that the four-step learning loop is completed. Often, learning comes to a halt after the "gaining knowledge" stage.

For example, say the legal team at a company wants all its employees to go through a training course on ethics. The employees duly take the online or classroom training class where they are lectured on the ethics of accepting gifts from vendors. If the employees are paying attention, they may have obtained knowledge and even understood why it is not appropriate to accept gifts from clients. But then what? Will they ever get an opportunity to apply this knowledge or reflect on it? Typically not. And even if they do, they will be less likely to remember it at the time when they most need it.

Training courses can only go so far to promote learning, and, in most cases, they don't even transfer critical information into the minds of potentially bored or disengaged employees. Surely, there must be a better way.

As some organizations are demonstrating, there is a better way. For example, telecommunications company Ericsson holds a "Learning Week," during which employees can learn from others and teach what they know. People can sign up for sessions that they want to teach others about and either participate in the program online through collaboration tools or at an in-person meeting. For Ericsson, Learning Week has become a wildly successful strategy to encourage peer-to-peer learning. This is because the people sharing their expertise gain as much as the peers who participate.

The strategy for peer-to-peer learning isn't to lecture, but to set up the learning so there is an opportunity to have meaningful conversations, to listen to different points of view, to get feedback, and to reflect. If we take the earlier example of the legal team, a learning session could include a discussion with peers about difficult ethical situations where peers could share their experiences with legal issues and also include a peer legal expert there to answer questions.

Peer-to-Peer Learning at LinkedIn

In 2014, Kelly's team at LinkedIn designed a social, collaborative, peer-to-peer learning program called "Conscious Business" in partnership with Fred Kofman, based on the content from his book *Conscious Business: How to Build Value through Values.*[10]

Conscious Business is a term to describe people who express their own values through work. The idea behind the Conscious Business learning program was to help LinkedIn employees understand how to apply the company's culture and values in a practical way on the job. This was a tough message to impart, given that company values tend to be somewhat nebulous and therefore difficult to put into practice. Realistically, how could employees demonstrate company values such as "integrity" during their day-to-day working lives? That was the challenge.

In designing the learning program, the team focused on three LinkedIn values, correlating to the theories in Kofman's book:[11]

"Conscious Business"	LinkedIn Values
Authentic Communication	Be open, honest, and constructive
Impeccable Coordination	Relationships matter
Constructive Negotiation	Take intelligent risks

The program was four weeks, cohort-based, and would take a commitment of three to four hours per week for participants. It started off as invitation-only, making it selective before being rolled out to the entire LinkedIn employee base. The strategy worked—soon there was a waiting list of people who wanted to get into the program.

Once in the program, participants were confronted with real-world situations during a variety of practice sessions. For example, finding yourself in a difficult conversation at work is very common. One assignment began by asking participants to think of a real-life difficult conversation they wanted to have at work but were possibly avoiding. Once they had an idea in mind, they were shown several short videos featuring Kofman role-playing scenarios that demonstrated how to tackle difficult conversations.

For instance, one of the participants, John, wanted to have a real conversation with one of his employees, Mark, about missing important deadlines and how that behavior was impacting the team. Before he spoke to Mark, he was guided by one of Kofman's videos to practice with one of his peers. John was also prompted to write out a simple script of what he wanted to say to Mark, together with possible responses based on what he thought Mark might say. The goal of the conversation was to be "open, honest, and constructive." Eventually, John had the conversation with Mark and it didn't go as well as John wanted. John felt awkward providing negative feedback to Mark and felt that Mark was defensive in his responses.

Once everyone in the group had a chance to practice a difficult conversation, they then went to an online discussion group to share with their peers what had happened in the practice session. This is where John got an opportunity to talk about how his discussion with Mark went. This became a very powerful learning tool because it gave participants a chance to reflect on what happened. For instance, they could ask themselves and others if the conversation had gone well, and if so, why? Had the feedback session been awkward or contentious? How had John and Mark handled it? By sharing these reflections with their peers, who were all going through the same exercise, they were able to understand how others handled the situation, and what they did well or could do better next time. Sharing feedback and experiences in this way meant that the participants were gaining real insights from their peers as well as building relationships with them.

The Conscious Business program turned out to be the most popular learning program offered at LinkedIn and went on to win some learning awards. The participants were learning great concepts, like the importance of building relationships at work. In addition, they were actively practicing what they had learned on the job and seeing real results.

In 2015, not long after the Conscious Business program, Kelly's team set up another initiative called "Learning Labs"—a pop-up, physical learning area during lunch hour where employees could stop by and get help with topics related to their roles (similar to a drop-in IT desk). For example, employees could access something called the "Transformation Plan," which helped them focus on their career goals and tie learning to the skills they wanted to develop. If employees wanted help talking through their Transformation Plan, a group of learning professionals would staff the learning lab and help people one-on-one and peer-to-peer. Employees could also take part in group learning sessions to get suggestions on how to improve their own profiles on LinkedIn. Let's face it, if you're a LinkedIn employee, you really need to have an amazing profile.

As the LinkedIn example shows, the key to a successful peer-to-peer learning program is to ensure everyone taking part has a real goal or problem to solve. Some organizations run peer-to-peer programs that have theoretical problems to resolve, in the hope that participants will apply the same model to a real problem when or if it arises on the job. This approach really doesn't work as well. Think about it—do busy employees really want to take time out from their real jobs to work on a theoretical problem? The chances are the task will either be completed reluctantly or take a back seat to other, more real priorities.

On the other hand, being assigned a real work problem as a learning opportunity is powerful. Employees become motivated to participate in a problem they can relate to and are accountable for and take the necessary time to resolve it. They are getting work done with the added benefit of learning something new at the same time.

Building a Safe Environment for Peer-to-Peer Learning

For peer-to-peer learning to work, the participants need to feel safe enough to share their thoughts with their peers. This type of learning involves being open and vulnerable enough to accept constructive input and having the courage to give honest feedback rather than telling people what they want to hear. Receiving feedback involves keeping an open mind and appreciating that the other person has taken the time to think about how you can be better or do something better. Ideally, feedback should be perceived as a generous gesture that should be met with gratitude, rather than defensiveness.

While Google's Casap believes that exchanging honest feedback is a key part of peer-to-peer learning, he acknowledges it's not an easy concept to apply:

> *There is an old saying "be careful when someone asks you for feedback, because what they are really looking for is validation." So if you show me an article you are writing for a magazine and you ask me to review it for you, I'm usually going to give it back to you with some statements like "it was well written," or "don't take it personally," or, "I just have a couple of edits." I might not even dive deep because I don't want to offend you or make you feel bad about what you wrote versus really giving you feedback and really giving you assessments. So, this idea of peer-to-peer starts at this level with an understanding and appreciation that real collaboration is the ability to ask good questions, the ability to give good feedback and take good feedback, the ability to assess someone and be assessed, the ability to influence and to build consensus. Those types of things we really need to build and we're not doing that in education.[12]*

As Casup says, constructive feedback is where the real value is. There is no better way of learning how we're functioning and what we can do better.

Yet, many people struggle to be open enough to provide honest feedback, especially in an environment where they don't feel safe. According to research by Ruth Helyer, professor of work-based learning at Leeds Trinity University,

> *[Learning] is most effective when it involves others and as a consequence the chance to collaborate and share ideas about changes, alterations and new ways of operating. Reflecting critically, and sharing the outcomes of this, can be frightening and can cause feelings of vulnerability amongst those exposing their thoughts and findings; working in groups and*

networks with fellow workers or other students can offer the support and multiple input needed to help deal with this and provide evidence that the process is worthwhile, even if it feels daunting at first.[13]

Google discovered this when it embarked on Project Aristotle, a quest to find out why some teams succeed where others falter.[14] Over the course of two years, 180 teams were analyzed. It turned out that successful teams were not just about putting the best people together, as Google had previously thought, or about shared educational backgrounds or hobbies, but rather about team dynamics. The members of the most successful teams trusted each other enough to take risks and shared the same sense of confidence that they would not be mocked, embarrassed, or punished for expressing themselves in front of their peers. As one Google engineer told the researchers when speaking about his team leader, "[He] is direct and straightforward, which creates a safe space for you to take risks."[15]

The findings led Google researchers to conclude that psychological safety, or a shared belief that team members feel safe enough to express themselves honestly and openly without fear of judgment or retribution, was the key ingredient in binding team members together. When people feel psychologically safe in a working environment, they will be more likely to communicate more openly, share knowledge, raise concerns and report mistakes, and actively seek and provide constructive feedback. As Google discovered, showing empathy, listening to each other, being sensitive to feelings and needs, and engaging in emotional conversations normally shied away from in the workplace are key to productive working relationships among peers.

Google works hard to promote the idea of psychological safety within peer-to-peer learning. Tech Talks, for instance, are where engineers share their knowledge with their peers regarding new, cutting-edge technology in a series of in-house presentations. In these talks, the engineers talk about their projects and show how they solve problems with technology. The presenting engineers set aside ample time for questions and answers from their peers, providing a safe space to learn and share information. The Tech Talks are so popular that they have been recorded and posted on a YouTube channel hosted by Google called "Google Tech

Talks" (sometimes known as "TED for geeks") and shared with engineers worldwide.[16]

Like Google, many companies have adopted a similar peer-to-peer learning model. Since 2013, computer software company Adobe has fully embraced peer-to-peer learning through its "Leaders Teaching Leaders" program for senior leaders.[17] As part of the program, Adobe partners with UC Berkeley's Haas School of Business to facilitate solving real business problems. According to one participant, Francis,

> *If there's one teacher at the front of the room, telling everyone how to lead, participants get only one perspective. But if we bring together all of our incredible human assets to teach each other and share [our] experiences, we all benefit. The primary asset that a company has is its people, and this is the best way to maximize the value of that asset.[18]*

Francis also reinforces that reflection is a big part of Adobe's "Leaders Teaching Leaders" program.

> *I learned that it's important to share not just techniques but also thinking processes with your peers. This is an environment that allows those interactions to happen and those stories to come up. When I faced this situation, how did I handle it? What wisdom can others find in my experience? If we can all tap into each other's knowledge and experience, we can all help each other become stronger leaders. I've always believed in the power of sharing, and the [program] just reinforced that sharing experiences with up-and-coming leaders is a powerful way to help them lead their own teams more effectively.[19]*

Building Peer Recognition

While Google is busy cultivating a healthy peer-to-peer learning environment through its focus on psychological safety, airline JetBlue is going one step further. The airline has partnered with social recognition company Globoforce to initiate a social "peer-to-peer" recognition program.[20] As part of the program, coworkers can nominate each other for their work effort and valuable contribution. The person receiving the most nominations is rewarded with points that they can either spend on a small reward, such as dinner, or save for bigger rewards, like vacations or cruises. The result? A 2 percent increase in employee engagement and a 3 percent increase in retention for every 10 percent of employees who received recognition.

But the results don't stop there. JetBlue also discovered that higher engagement had a positive impact on customer satisfaction and loyalty. In other words, employees who were engaged were three times more likely to "wow" customers, according to favorable customer feedback. Because its employees feel valued, recognized, and appreciated, JetBlue has a thriving peer-to-peer sharing culture.

MBA and Peer-to-Peer Learning

The MBA has been long regarded as the "Holy Grail" of business education. An MBA is typically a two-year, full-time program costing over $50,000 on average and upwards of $100,000 at top schools. The theory is that an MBA is the shortcut to getting a job with a higher salary; yet realistically, how many people have the time and money to take two years out of their professional career to complete an MBA?

However, there are alternatives for those who don't have the time and money to dedicate to being a full-time, or even part-time, MBA student. In 2009, former GE CEO Jack Welch started an online MBA program called The Jack Welch Management Institute (JWMI) that offers a fully online program where all students and professors are remote. JWMI takes roughly two and a half years to complete, and at just under $40,000, it costs one-third to one-half less than other MBA programs It also has been named by *CEO Magazine* as one of the top 15 global online MBA programs for 2017, and one of the top 25 MBA programs by the *Princeton Review*.[21]

According to Welch, the program is a practical way for students to apply what they have learned to real-work situations. The flow is "Learn it on Monday, apply it on Tuesday, and share it on Friday." Students communicate about assignments in forums, chat rooms, and over e-mail. Some may argue that's not as effective as building in-person relationships, but it can still be very effective. In addition to a peer-to-peer component, the program gives students a "success coach," in addition to discussions once a quarter led by Welch himself.

Seth Godin, best-selling author and entrepreneur, has also created an alternative to getting an MBA, called the altMBA.[22] It is an intensive four-week online leadership and management workshop for high-performing individuals who want to "level up and lead." Participants are divided into learning groups of five peers (which change on a weekly basis) to work together on weekly projects. After each assignment, participants are asked to give feedback on each other's work. This creates a vibrant learning environment where everyone is held accountable for their contributions.

The altMBA process follows the peer-to-peer learning model outlined earlier in this chapter. Learning groups are first given a real problem to solve, and then they give feedback to their peers, before finally engaging in self-reflection on what has been learned and how the problem/project might be approached differently next time.

It costs $3,000 and involves using digital tools such as Slack (a team communication service) and Zoom (video and web conferencing software) to connect with about 100 students each session from all over the world. In 2016, students from 27 countries participated in the program. The program has had leaders from top companies like Nike, Whole Foods, Google, Microsoft, Hallmark, and Coca-Cola.

Media solutions consultant and altMBA participant Brigitte Cutshall likens the course to a "tough sailing adventure" but feels that the experience was transformational.[23] She learned how to think critically by "[asking] WHY first when faced with a decision" and to "focus on what's important and not just urgent stuff." More importantly, the course created a long-lasting bond with her fellow participants, whom she keeps in touch with daily. In four weeks, Cutshall had a thriving network thanks to her engagement in peer-to-peer learning.

Joanne Heyman, founder and CEO of Heyman Partners and adjunct professor at Columbia University, shared her experience with peer-to-peer learning. Heyman is internationally recognized as a thought leader, innovator, and key adviser within the social innovation sector. When Joanne signed up for the altMBA in September 2016, she had been a solo practitioner for six years. Much as she enjoyed working for herself, she realized that working alone had its limitations. She felt altMBA would be a really great opportunity for her to interact with people, gain insights, work in a community, and find new ways in which to grow and structure her business.

Like Brigitte, she found the experience exhilarating, and was particularly impressed by the caliber of her fellow participants and the quality of feedback she received:

> *I feel like I benefited from some really honest feedback to my ideas; I liked being pushed to go deeper and to be more detailed. Frequently when I'm trying to do things for myself, I don't do that. I can do it for my clients, but I can't do it for myself. So, I found it incredibly useful to be asked thoughtful and thought-provoking questions on a regular basis—mostly from my peers in the program and sometimes from the facilitators.*[24]

By the end of the program, Heyman was convinced that she wanted to work as a collective rather than by herself, but the outcome didn't turn out as she expected.

> *I came out of the program very, very enthusiastic about the power of collaboration, and thought about turning my practice into a collective. I tried for about four to five months and it didn't work. And out of those failed experiments came a much deeper and more confident commitment to developing myself with others rather than feeling like I had to be institutionally surrounded by other people. So at the end, it was an incredibly powerful experience; it just didn't end up the way I thought it would.*[25]

Both Cutshall and Heyman learned the value of working with peers from all different backgrounds and countries over the course of just a few weeks. Imagine the wealth of knowledge that could be gained if that level of peer learning occurred every single day in organizations.

Learning with Peers (Over Beers)

On the first Tuesday of every month, Dutch psychologist-turned-designer Wouter de Bres meets with his fellow design peers to swap ideas over a few beers. On the surface, it looks like a social event, but for de Bres this gathering is one of the most important parts of his learning experience.

De Bres is the founder of two companies in the Netherlands: digital agency Bread & Pepper; and Gibbon, an online knowledge-sharing platform. He credits his peers for his success: "I have learned more about design from my peers than I have from design courses or books."[26]

But de Bres does not confine himself to solely in-person peer events; he is also a member of Dribbble, an online social network for designers. Through this online platform, de Bres is able to not only showcase his work, but also receive feedback from professional designers he admires.

"The feedback is honest," he says, "and could be perceived as a bit harsh, but for me it is invaluable. Besides, all the designers on Dribbble follow the same code: 'Don't take it personally; you are not your design.'"[27]

This understanding helps to foster trust and honesty within the design community. As de Bres explains, "The great thing is that we can receive critical feedback and still go out for a friendly beer if we happen to meet in person one day. We are helping each other while also learning from each other."

Twitter also played a huge role when it came to learning from and communicating with peers—de Bres would read every article and book recommended by designers to further enhance his learning, and he regularly connected with some great design contacts. This process of sharing knowledge even became the main source of inspiration for knowledge-sharing start-up Gibbon. But to get Gibbon off the ground, de Bres needed funding. When de Bres and his team landed a spot in an investor accelerator program in 2012, de Bres had a chance to spend some time in Silicon Valley and was determined to make the most of his opportunity.

I was in Silicon Valley for 60 days, so I set myself a goal to meet at least one designer per day, most of whom I had connected with through Twitter but had yet to meet in person. It was incredible how much I learned. One designer would immediately introduce me to another designer they knew, and so it went until I had well over 60 design contacts.[28]

De Bres' contacts turned out to be top designers from Airbnb, Facebook, Google, Twitter, Yahoo!, Square, ZenDesk, and Flipboard, to name just a few. Through his passion for learning from his peers, de Bres has managed to build up an enviable professional network populated with talented designers whom he continues to collaborate with and learn from every day.

As de Bres' experience shows, we can learn faster and progress more quickly by harnessing the knowledge shared by our peers. Worrying about problems doesn't make any sense when we have so many people around to help and advise us. There are so many advantages to learning from our peers both at work and worldwide. All we need to do is take part.

Key Skills for Peer-to-Peer Learning

Peer-to-peer learning gives us three key skills: the skill of self-reflection, the skill of giving and receiving feedback, and the skill of critical thinking. This section focuses on how we can refine those skills to enhance our own learning experience.

How to self-reflect

People tend *not* to engage in self-reflection for several reasons. They either don't understand how it works, or they don't like the thought of taking the necessary time out from their busy day, or they don't like the idea of assessing their own actions and potential areas of weakness.

However, like all good skills, self-reflection requires commitment and practice. Anybody can engage in self-reflection if they practice a few simple steps:[29]

1. Reflect on your day and ask yourself some questions

- What might you be avoiding?
- How are you helping others to achieve their goals?
- How might you be helping or hindering other people's progress?
- What is your most frustrating working relationship? How might you be contributing to it?
- Think of the last meeting you had. How could you have been more effective?

2. Choose the best method for you to reflect

The method of reflection is up to the individual. If you are the type of person who prefers to gather your thoughts alone, then by all means grab a journal and write down your thoughts or go for a walk or a bike ride. However, self-reflection does not have to be a solitary activity. It is entirely possible to reflect with a colleague, a coach, or a mentor, as long as you're reflecting constructively on the matter rather than complaining about it.

3. Make time for self-reflection

Schedule reflection time in the same way you would schedule a meeting—put it in your calendar. Deliberately making space for it is more likely to motivate you to actually do it.

4. Set your own time frame

Some people reflect for an hour; others, a few minutes. If an hour seems too much in the beginning, then try 10 minutes. Giving yourself a manageable amount of time to commit in the first instance still helps you make progress.

5. Think about your thinking

Analyze your thoughts and think about your own perspectives and why you are thinking in a particular way. Do you agree with all your thoughts? If not, why?

How to enhance your critical thinking skills

Critical thinking is fundamental to problem-solving and decision-making. The good news is that all of us can become excellent critical thinkers if we ask the right questions. Here are some good critical thinking questions to ask yourself when someone assigns to you a tough challenge:

- What does this problem mean?
- How should I interpret what has been said?
- Does my interpretation make sense? Is it logical?
- What assumptions/conclusions should I draw?
- What additional information do I need to resolve this problem?
- How many ways can this problem be resolved?
- Do I have enough supporting information/facts to make a decision?
- Is the information credible?
- If I decide, what are the consequences of that decision in the short term and the long term?
- Who else can I talk to about this issue? What other perspectives can I seek?

How to give and receive constructive feedback

One of the most important skills we learn from peer-to-peer learning is how to give and accept feedback. Neither is easy to do, but with practice it becomes a great way to empower ourselves and others. Remember, exchanging feedback is a two-way street, so make sure you are giving the other person enough time to react to what is being said, and allow dialogue where appropriate. The most successful feedback is based on clear communication and understanding. The following is a list of suggestions for giving and receiving constructive feedback:

1. Don't make it personal

When you're giving feedback, focus on the behavior, not the character. For example, if you're frustrated by a peer who is constantly late to meetings, don't attack the person ("You have a problem with time-keeping"), but instead make a helpful suggestion about how the behavior can be changed ("We can all kick off the discussion and finish more quickly when everyone is here at the same time").

2. Do be prepared

It may sound obvious, but if you're going to provide feedback, prepare what you're going to say before you say it. Stay on topic and make sure you use specific examples and references. Never generalize or expect someone to pick up on "hints." Successful feedback is based on clear communication between both parties.

3. Don't make comparisons

When you're providing feedback, be careful not to compare performances ("Look at Janet; she's never late!"). Comparing people with each other only breeds negative competition and resentment. However, you can compare past performance against current performance, as long as it doesn't involve anyone else.[30]

4. Do accept feedback with grace and dignity

Think of feedback as a positive way of empowering you to do better. Listen to understand what the other person is saying, summarize what you have heard, and ask plenty of questions to clarify your understanding. The person providing the feedback will be grateful to you for making such an effort to listen to what they are saying.

5. Don't be defensive

When you're receiving feedback, try to control your defensiveness. Being defensive or notably upset only makes the person giving feedback more uncomfortable. It also means that person will no longer view you as approachable and may stop giving you feedback altogether.

6. Do have some patience

It can be tempting to try to justify feedback that you perceive as unfair, but make sure you let the other person finish before you make your case. Similarly, it doesn't pay to argue. Try to control the impulse to jump in, and focus on taking the time to understand exactly what is being said before formulating a considered response.[31]

Building a successful peer-to-peer learning environment

Creating a successful peer-to-peer learning environment takes time, but plenty of organizations have managed to achieve it by following these guidelines:

- Appoint someone to *facilitate* the learning process. People who have typically been instructors in instructor-led training programs are often great facilitators. Peer learning facilitators make sure everyone stays on topic, notes key ideas and themes, and keeps the conversation moving forward.
- Focus on real-world situations by giving the group a real problem to solve. The key to a successful peer-to-peer learning program

is to ensure everyone taking part is engaged in something authentic to resolve.

- Build a safe peer-to-peer learning environment where participants feel comfortable enough to share their thoughts openly with their peers. Encourage empathy, active listening, sensitivity to feelings and needs, and engagement in emotional conversations.
- Promote peer-to-peer learning by holding inclusive events and conferences in person or online.
- Encourage peer-to-peer networking by setting up online social networks, organizing networking events, or setting up informal learning groups that meet regularly and exchange ideas (even over a few beers!).

CHAPTER SIX

Succeed with the Right Technology

M ANY COMPANIES CHOOSE technology before really understanding how it can address the business problems they are trying to solve. For example, someone thought it would be a great idea to take a classroom lecture and put it online. But, think about the worst professor you ever had in high school or college, and imagine putting his lectures on YouTube. Although you have the technology to distribute a terrible lecture to millions of people, not many people will find this useful, inspiring, or engaging. If it wasn't good in the first place, adding technology is not going to make it any better. In another case, an elementary school teacher bought every student in her class an iPad thinking that technology would improve learning. But she didn't really have a plan for how they would use the iPads. Companies, too, often buy technology before they know how they're going to use it. It may sound obvious, but it is far more beneficial to assess the problem first and then choose the right technology to address it.

As learning scientist Bror Saxberg says, "Technology does nothing for learning. What technology does is take either a good learning solution or a bad learning solution and make it more affordable, more reliable, more available, more data rich, and more personalized."[1] In other words, technology is useless if you don't start with a solid foundation and strategy for what you want to do with learning.

In this chapter, we'll discuss some of the most common business challenges companies are facing today and how technology can help solve those issues. We will also explore some of the most innovative education technologies in the market, including those that enable you to explore and create career goals, help people find their purpose at work, and help individuals and companies understand what skills people have and need. We'll look at technology for practicing skills, learning in teams, and solving real-world business problems. In summary, we'll dive into the following technologies to show you how they can enhance your strategy. Do you want to help your employees:

- Explore or create career goals? (Fuel50)
- Understand/find their purpose at work? (Imperative)
- Understand the skills people have and the skills they need? (Degreed)
- Practice and get feedback about their skills? (Practice)
- Work in teams to solve business problems? (Intrepid)

We can make sense of it all if we start with "Why?" Why do you need the technology? What problem are you trying to solve?

Building Bicycles of the Mind

Technology is forcing people to fundamentally rethink the way they do their jobs. The reality is that we can no longer separate learning from work. Nigel Paine, learning thought leader and author of *The Learning Challenge*, talks about efficiency and productivity in the workforce. He believes lapses in employee productivity are caused by lack of investment in our own learning. Paine says, "Learning, for sure, increases human productivity. It not only motivates people, but it gives them new ways of doing things. And new ways of doing things are generally more efficient ways of doing things."[2]

To reinforce his point, Paine recalls the famous story that Steve Jobs told in the early days of Apple when he likened computers to bicycles for our minds. Jobs said that on their own, humans are not the most efficient creatures, but when you give humans a bicycle, they become the most efficient species on the planet: "That is what a computer is to me—it's the most remarkable tool we've ever come up with. It's the equivalent of a bicycle for our minds."[3]

Paine fully believes in the power of Jobs' theory. "This notion of computers and technology as a bicycle for our minds is very important because it means that it's not about content. It's about process, and about the 'apps' world where things plug into each other, to solve tasks and solve problems."[4]

So over time, when better technology is developed, we get rid of the old and adopt the new, and in doing so we can increase the effectiveness, productivity, and the process of work and people.

But just because technology is better doesn't mean it's the right choice. Choosing the best learning technology for your organization means figuring out the type of help your employees need to advance their careers through learning. Once you have that information, you can then find the technology that can make the solution more affordable, more available, and more personalized.

Explore or Create Career Goals

Anne Fulton grew up in Auckland, New Zealand, and studied organization psychology as well as guidance counseling. She's had a lifelong passion to help people make great career decisions, to guide them on their career journeys, and to help people think more intently about where they want their professional careers to go.

Her own career journey led her to become a vocational guidance counselor and then an organizational psychologist, where she built predictive career and recruitment tests. She then went on to start several tech companies—all focusing on professional development and careers. In 2011, Fulton and her co-founder, Jo Mills, created career pathing software solution Fuel50 with the mission of creating a meaningful workplace for people around the globe. The idea of fueling passion helped inform part of their company name.

Fulton describes Fuel50 as "Match.com meets LinkedIn."[5] In other words, it matches people with career paths and internal opportunities and then connects them to others within the company who can help them succeed. The concept behind Fuel50 is timely—research shows that 46 percent of employees want more visible career pathways within their organizations.[6] This is because they want to know if there's a path for growth, development, and career progression at their current company. So, if you want employees to grow their careers inside your company, you need to connect them to opportunities available internally. Unfortunately, it's often easier just to look externally at new opportunities through LinkedIn.

Fuel50 helps employees find the answers to questions such as:

- What am I best suited to here in this business?
- What role could I aspire to?
- How can I get from where I am today to where I want to be?
- How can I grow my career here in this business?
- How can I find a mentor, coach, or learning experience (stretch assignment, projects, and part-time assignments known as "gigs") to help me grow my career?
- In essence, what would I do if I could do anything?

Fuel50 is also valuable to managers and leaders because it gives people a reality check by equipping them with a "career match score." As Fulton says, "We believe anyone can do anything if they want to, but we will give them a current potential match score to their target role and the road map in terms of competencies, skills, qualifications, and experiences they will need to get to where they want to go."

One of the main goals of Fuel50 is to build a continuous growth culture and mindset within the business. This is particularly valuable for millennials. Let's take new hire Rashid as an example. Rashid joined your company six months ago, straight from school, as a business analyst with an MBA. He wants to understand what is required to become the CFO. When he goes through Fuel50, he is told that he has the potential to become CFO, but right now his match is 18 percent. Then he is provided with a road map to follow with some stepping-stones along the way. This kind of visibility is something employees hunger for, along with an understanding of how they can live their values, purpose, and passion at work. These components are all important parts of the Fuel50 experience.

The product has since morphed into a career path tool. It's designed to help people achieve their full potential and leverage their talents through career insight identifiers known as "FuelFactors," which cover values, talents, work/style fit, and career agility. Career factors are matched to job opportunities within the company, and employees are supported in finding gigs, stretch assignments, and mentors to assist their career growth.

MasterCard is a good example of a company that has activated career pathing across the globe for their people using Fuel50. MasterCard initially introduced Fuel50 as a career development initiative to help their "Managers Matter" coaching program. It's become popular within the company; Fuel50 is now being used by 12,000 employees globally. Elizabeth Barrieros, director at MasterCard, says:

> In the future, we hope to continue to build enhancements into the platform that will allow our employees to build mentoring relationships, get feedback on their talents from others in the organization, and continue to build their network. Additionally, we are looking into integrating Fuel50 with Degreed so that our employees can directly access learning resources that are related to the talents they want to further develop.[7]

Bringing Purpose to Work

Aaron Hurst started his first business when he was 16 years old and has been an entrepreneur ever since. When Hurst was in college at the University of Michigan, he developed an influential program in partnership with the university that took students to correctional facilities to teach creative writing to inmates. Hurst believed that experiential learning was so much more valuable than learning from books. Having a learning disability himself, he never learned very well from books; he learned by doing. From his experience of visiting inmates, he discovered insights on a multitude of topics, from creative writing to sociology, from psychology to criminal justice, and from group dynamics to empathy. This led Hurst to realize the value of experiential learning as a powerful way to absorb information and to show how life really works.

In 1995, Hurst moved into the nonprofit world, working on inner-city education in Chicago. While he loved what nonprofits were doing, he quickly realized that they had given up on having a big impact because they bought into the poverty mentality of nonprofits, meaning they could only take their ventures so far because of their financial limitations. So, Hurst decided to focus on what companies did to scale, especially for-profit startups, and try to apply that to the nonprofit world.

He began that journey by moving to Silicon Valley in 1997 and landed a job at a real-estate startup as a product manager educating consumers so that they could take control and ownership of the home-buying process. He then went to another startup, iSyndicate (later acquired by content analytics company YellowBrix), which syndicated and distributed content, and was a precursor to blogging. What he learned by working at two tech startups was that the issue at nonprofits was partly about money, but more importantly, it was about not having access to the same talent. To really scale a company, Hurst believed in hiring ahead of its needs; nonprofits were always hiring way behind their needs. Typically, those startups didn't have resources in marketing, technology, HR, or other functions. They were always just surviving.

Hurst knew that people were drawn to philanthropy and volunteering, but realized that there wasn't a good way to connect talent in areas that were needed most in nonprofits. He also saw that companies weren't taking advantage of the experiential parts of learning. So, in 2001, he decided to connect the two by starting a company called the Taproot Foundation.[8] Taproot's mission is to lead, mobilize, and engage professionals in pro bono service that drives social change. Taproot connects the skills of all types of professionals to help nonprofits with the talent they need ahead of the curve. In 12 years, Hurst scaled the pro-bono social movement into a $15 billion-dollar marketplace.

For Hurst, one of the most rewarding things about Taproot was the number of people who told him that doing pro bono work was the most fulfilling part of their career. This feedback also made him think about the flip side of that statement—that people were fundamentally dissatisfied with their careers and tended to supplement their jobs with volunteer work to find meaning and purpose.

Hurst spent the past few decades exploring the relationship between purpose and work, so in 2013 he decided to embark on a new journey, co-founding the technology company Imperative. The goal of this company is to imagine a world where the *majority* of the workforce is purpose-oriented[9] because of the huge benefits to employees, companies, and society.

To create awareness around purpose at work, Hurst published *The Purpose Economy: How Your Desire for Impact, Personal Growth and Community Is Changing the World*.[10] In his book, he details his extensive research on how people perceive work. What Hurst discovered is that people are wired to see work from two different viewpoints. The first is through purpose orientation, meaning that some people view work as a way to achieve personal fulfillment as well as a method of serving others. In the second orientation, people view work as a way to achieve status, advancement, and income.

Hurst's philosophy is that the economy is changing, and he also emphasizes that when we apply rigor to purpose, it becomes an economic driver. Imperative built the first ever assessment around purpose so that people could learn about themselves, and then expanded it so that people could build their careers around their purpose drivers. So instead of dreaming to be a great engineer or a great salesperson, you can think about how to become outstanding at your purpose. The thing is that no matter what job or role you have, your purpose makes you feel incredible and fulfilled—it's the one thing that is sustainable.

Hurst sees an urgent need in companies to create a more purposeful work culture. "Companies across industries are hungry to evolve beyond engagement and are inspired to embrace fulfillment as the framework for their talent strategies."[11] Imperative is working with Fortune 100 companies to help employees think about skills development, career development, and leadership development through the lens of purpose. It helps people look at the competencies they should be building regardless of the job they have. This is going to become even more important for future generations. In Imperative's study, *Purpose in Higher Education*,[12] Generation Z is the most purpose-oriented group to enter the workforce yet; 47 percent are purpose-oriented (compared to 28 percent in the workforce now), and nearly a third of students say they would rather major in a purpose than a subject.

To determine purpose-orientation at the company level, employees take an assessment that determines their purpose drivers and answer questions about how fulfilled they are in their work. The information they share provides a good measure of their relationships, their impact, and their sense of growth. Participants are also asked to set a 90-day career goal; this could something like being a better leader or manager, or if the participant is new to the company, the goal could be based on their first 90 days on the job. Depending on the assessment results, employees are given their purpose drivers and a dashboard that sets out their short-term goals, the actions they need to take every week, and their personalized results measuring relationships, impact, and growth. Building on that technology platform, Imperative has started to partner with external coaches certified in the Imperative methodology to help guide people on how they can realize their purpose at work.

Why Should CEOs and Companies Care about Purpose?

Some companies balk at thinking about purpose and meaning at work, but there's good reason for leaders to care. According to the 2015[13] Workforce Purpose Index sponsored by New York University, workers with a purpose-orientation are the most valuable and highest potential segment of the workforce, regardless of industry or role. On every measure, purpose-oriented workers have better outcomes than their peers:

- 20 percent longer expected tenure
- 50 percent more likely to be in leadership positions
- 47 percent more likely to be promoters of their employers
- 64 percent higher levels of fulfillment in their work

Understand the Skills Employees Have and the Skills They Need

David has had a lofty purpose for a few decades now—a goal that challenges the way we think about learning and education. He's been on a mission to "jailbreak the degree" and change the way the world learns and give everyone credit for all the learning they do throughout their professional careers and indeed their lifetime. In 2012, David put that goal into motion and co-founded the education technology company Degreed.

Growing up, David was a good student, investing a lot of time and energy in studying to make sure he kept his 4.0 GPA, and took as many college prep classes as he could handle. He was yearbook editor and on the student council, played soccer, held an after-school job, was an Eagle Scout, and played the saxophone. In short, David did all the things he was "supposed to do" to be that quintessential college applicant. But the truth was, as good a student as David was, his approach to education and learning was simply a means to an end. He believed in the narrative told to him and his fellow classmates—that doing well in school would lead to being accepted into the best university, which would in turn lead to the best jobs after graduation and set them up for the best career—"best" always meaning the safest and most prestigious choice.

However, after taking the ACT when he was 17 years old, he had an epiphany. He realized that despite the years of time and effort he had invested in his education, how he scored on this one test would determine nearly half of his future—it was half of the equation for what university he would get into, which in turn seemed half of the equation for what job opportunities would be available. To him, the system seemed crazy.

Although David didn't know it at the time, college marketing dollars are dictated by SAT scores, ACT scores, and your zip code—that's how universities target potential students. It's not because you were good at math or were in band; it was because you scored high on the ACT.

David says, "I believe that high-stakes testing, like the ACT or the SAT, doesn't have anything to do with who you are or what your potential is. In fact, it's strongly correlated simply with your socioeconomic status at the time of taking the test. The education system incentivizes people to master test taking, not how to learn." David realized that while he had become a great student, he was actually a really terrible learner. He had no passion for learning or sense of curiosity, and he placed little value in what he was taught. He had been programmed to soak up information and spit it back out on tests. David decided that more than being a great student, what he really aspired to was to be a great learner. That goal cemented his passion for lifelong learning.

Despite his reservations about how high-stakes testing operated, David stayed on the conveyor belt and took the tests and did well. He graduated from Brigham Young University with a degree in economics, and, like many others, his degree became the currency by which his value was determined in the job market.

Coming out of university, he was offered a job by a management consulting firm in Dallas, but despite learning a lot, enhancing his skills, and working with great people, he felt something was missing. During this time, he realized that he needed to dedicate his energy and his career to his passion for education, even if it meant giving up the prestige and financial security of management consulting.

David recalls, "I started to think about the ways our formal education is not representative of who we are or what we can do. More importantly, I realized that it should be our skills, irrespective or how or where we develop them, that should be what determines our opportunities, and I wanted to be part of the solution."

He started looking for people and companies doing interesting things in learning and education but didn't find much. Then he heard about a little tech start-up back in Utah called Zinch, which boasted the tagline "Students are more than a test score," and became intrigued. Zinch was akin to a LinkedIn for high school students where they created profiles that were accessible as part of the college admissions process. That way, the students were being evaluated on more than just their test scores.

David emailed the team at Zinch and they responded once or twice, but things weren't progressing fast enough for David. So he bought a plane ticket and flew out, unannounced, to their office. He knocked on their door and said, "Hey, I'm that guy you've been emailing with, can I take you to lunch?" By the time lunch was over, David had a job offer, which he accepted on the spot.

In retrospect, David admits the leap from prestige to purpose was hard. As a management consultant he had been well paid, was on a promising career track, and had excellent benefits. Joining Zinch meant a 60 percent pay cut, and a move into his parents' basement just weeks after the birth of his first baby.

In 2012, following three years of working for Zinch, David had cemented his vision on how to transform the educational system, and he was finally ready to start his own company. He started Degreed from San Francisco and, with a small team, developed the initial product: a platform to provide people and companies to track ALL lifelong learning and a profile that individuals could own that enabled them to track their learning throughout their entire career.

David realized that learning is a journey where we travel between universities, employers, and providers of education. You learn on YouTube, and perhaps on TED; listen to a podcast on your commute, then take training at work; maybe later you fly to a conference where you will read a book on the plane. You journey between many destinations and providers of education, and while the market has seen a lot of consumer-facing innovations in providing new ways to learn, no one had set out to support the learner on that journey as they travel between providers of education. Degreed set out to be the first platform that would support you with a continuous model of lifelong learning that helped you discover the best pathways of learning and get credit for everything you learned.

Now, years later, Degreed is one of the leading education technology companies in the world helping many of the Fortune 100 companies and beyond solve some of their most pressing business problems by identifying the skills of their employees and continuously helping employees upskill themselves.

At its core, Degreed is about helping people learn so they can build skills for both their personal and professional goals. Working in today's expertise economy you need to keep learning to stay relevant. By educating yourself on everything published on a specific topic, you can become one of the world's most knowledgeable experts on that topic. All it takes is an interest in learning and your disciplined commitment.

One quote, from Laszlo Bock, former Google head of HR, has always stayed with David: "When you look at people who don't go to school and make their way in the world, those are exceptional human beings."[14] David met one such exceptional person in the early days of Degreed who really had an impact on him. She was an accomplished woman in her mid-fifties but when he asked her to tell him about her education, she answered, "Oh, I'm not educated. I didn't go to university."

It really struck David that this woman still felt she was uneducated because she hadn't obtained a traditional degree. Practically speaking, what does a degree in economics 15 years ago tell you about what you know and can really do today? Degreed strives to reframe this lens by ensuring people are credited with all types of learning whether they have a degree or not.

Of course, David knew that unless our learning could be answered for, there really was no way for it to unlock opportunities. While people learn from a variety of sources throughout their lives, traditionally there hasn't been a way to track what was being learned or to take that learning with them when they changed jobs. Thanks to David's vision, anyone can now go to the Degreed website and set up a learning profile for free to start tracking their learning and continue to build the skills needed for their career goals. Through data and analytics, leaders and managers can also track their team and organizational learning goals and assess progress on building employees' skills to address the company's needs.

Practice Skills

Six years ago, Emily Foote[15] got a call from her former Drexel law professor, Karl Okamoto, who told her he had received a small six-month research grant to start an education company. To be eligible for this small business innovation research grant, the company would need to meet two goals: it had to have social impact and it had to create jobs. At the time, Foote was practicing law as a special education attorney, but Okamoto felt her experience in classroom teaching made her an ideal business partner.

Foote has always had a passion for education. Before practicing law, she spent two years as an elementary classroom teacher for underserved students in Atlanta through a program called Teach for America. Teach for America recruits exceptional college graduates from top universities around the country to spend two years teaching in the most disadvantaged schools before they embark on their lifelong career journey. After Teach for America, Foote spent an additional three years teaching high school and middle school at a KIPP charter school (tuition-free public school) before heading to law school. Both Teach for America and the KIPP charter schools programs were challenging the norms of a traditional education, which gave Foote excellent experience for the EdTech company she would join.

Part of her desire to make a difference through education was personal. While Foote always did well in high school, she never felt smart. Somehow, she always felt that she was fooling everyone and that she was just a very good mimic. In her opinion, traditional school is set up as a one-to-many scenario where a teacher or professor pushes content and hands out assignments. Although she felt she was a good student because she gave her professors what they asked for, she still wasn't sure that she absorbed all the content or learned what was most important. Even after getting good grades, she didn't feel smart or confident—that is, until she went to law school and took a class from one professor, Okamoto, who had a completely different approach to teaching and learning.

Okamoto was passionate about legal education, and he felt there was a disconnect between how law was being taught in law school and how much knowledge students were able to retain and apply in the real world after they graduated. Traditionally, law professors focused more on theory and not so much on practice. Through his own research, Okamoto discovered that law students took an average of eight years of practicing law before they became good, competent lawyers.

His research also showed that people who became competent lawyers benefited from being mentored, watching how peers and more experienced lawyers practiced law, practicing themselves, and getting feedback. In sum, lawyers needed practice, feedback, and reflection to excel in their profession, which, he thought, could be applied to other disciplines as well.

Okamoto decided to replicate in his law classes how he thought people really learned. It had a huge impact on his students. The model Okamoto developed involved chunking topics into four-week intervals. Classes were small—only 12 students. Week one focused on learning by doing; week two was about learning from peers; week three involved learning from experts in the field; and in week four there was an opportunity to reflect on what had been learned. The key to Okamoto's approach was not to begin teaching the students how to actually do something but to let the students figure that out for themselves.

For example, one four-week interval might involve learning about asset purchase sales agreements. But instead of giving a lecture on the topic, Okamoto would pair students up and give them one week to prepare an asset sale purchase agreement. Students then had to go away and figure out for themselves how to create one. The following week, each pair would present their completed assignment while the rest of the class scored them based on a rubric. This way, the presenting students were provided with feedback from their peers immediately after the presentation, through an open discussion of what they did well and what could have been better. Then the next pair would present until everyone demonstrated the skill, gave feedback, and received feedback.

In week three, the students would go on a field trip and visit a law firm to present their asset sales purchase agreements to two practicing attorneys and get feedback from those experts. To conclude the day, the two expert law partners would then demonstrate the skill to the students to show how it's done in the field. Week four was about reflection; each student had a journal and would write about what they learned, what they would do differently, and what they would keep doing. To finish week four, Okamoto would lead a retrospective discussion to synthesize all that had been learned during the four weeks. Then they would move on to the next topic. (Note that Okamoto's teaching closely follows the principles of the Learning Loop—knowledge, practice, feedback, and reflection—as discussed in chapter 1.)

After taking classes from Okamoto, Foote left law school feeling incredibly confident because she had had the opportunity to demonstrate true competence. So, when Okamoto told her that they could build a technology product that would mirror how he teaches, she felt excited. She realized the impact they could have on so many people and didn't hesitate to join her professor in the venture.

The company they founded, Practice, an EdTech company that provides peer-to-peer video coaching and assessment, would replicate through technology the process of how Okamoto taught in his classroom at Drexel University. Initially they wanted to leverage the power of video technology to help educators teach more effectively in the classroom, but they soon realized the potential in helping companies scale corporate learning through technology in a way that helps people learn and build skills in a practical, collaborative, powerful way by practicing.

When Emily and her team first talked to employees at large companies to understand how they liked to learn, most of them told her that they learned best through role-play, receiving feedback, being mentored, and interacting with their peers. But, as Foote discovered, most of the employees weren't learning this way at work. Managers didn't seem to have time to give the specific, actionable feedback their employees needed to hear. Because of all this, Emily felt even more confident that their product, Practice, would be a great solution for corporate learning.

"What Practice does is mimic these great, in-person small trainings that typically require a ton of time, money, and people, and allows companies to do it in a much more scalable way without degrading the efficacy simply because it's online for scalability purposes."[16]

Practice provides authoring tools (usually used by learning and development professionals) to build exercises that include the four learning steps and then delivers it to an intact working group. This means that the four components that make in-person training so effective are emulated in Practice:

1. A means to practice the skill
2. A way to build social capital and to get and give feedback from peers
3. A way to self-reflect
4. A way to get direct feedback from an "expert"

For example, pizza restaurant chain Dominos uses Practice for management training. They have an excellent ongoing management program where a few times a year, they fly people into headquarters to help them move up the leadership track. Some of the topics Dominos has focused on include how to manage a profit and loss statement (P&L), how to effectively give a direct report feedback, or how to set an agenda for a meeting. Since flying people into headquarters can be costly, not only from a travel expense perspective, but by taking people out of their day-to-day jobs, they've replaced one of the in-person, live trainings with Practice. As a result, Dominos saves on costs while retaining the effectiveness of the learning.

One of the largest global telecommunications and media companies is another example of a company using Practice, but they have adopted it for their customer support new hires. In the first instance, a group of new hires is given a set of exercises to complete, such as how to properly greet a customer, or how to handle a customer who is complaining about their bill. Firstly, new hires are shown a video of a customer upset about their bill. Then the new hire creates a video of how they think they should respond to the upset client. They then upload that video and in return get a set of assessment questions asking them to rate themselves on how they think they did in the interaction. If they don't like how they scored, they can re-record their video until they are satisfied with their own self-assessment. In other words, they can keep practicing until they get it right. On average, people resubmitted their videos six times before they were satisfied with their work.

During the second stage, the new hires engage in a crowd-sourced peer-review process. People are randomly assigned peers to review and they use the same assessment they used to rate themselves. According to the surveys conducted by Emily's team, people love getting and giving the peer feedback. They enjoy receiving feedback because they feel they learn more from their peers than their managers; their peers are the ones actually doing the job. They also enjoy giving feedback, some even providing it to more than the required three peers. Those surveyed said that providing feedback to others made them feel good because they felt that they were truly helping others.

But probably the most impactful part of the product, and what most inspired Emily to create Practice, is the chance for self-reflection. This is where the real learning happens. So in stage three, new hires get a "model" example of how they might have responded to an upset customer, or how they might have handled the difficult conversation. Both this example and the hire's own recorded video response are shown. Looking at the two in parallel initiates self-reflection. "What did I learn? What am I going to start doing? What am I going to stop doing?"

Self-reflection turns a traditional, passive model of education into something that insists you think about what you've learned. Instead of pretending that you "get it" or mimicking what you think someone wants without truly understanding, self-reflection helps people to absorb the information and gives them the confidence to master a new skill.

Work in Teams to Solve Business Problems

Sam Herring is a serial entrepreneur in Seattle and a self-confessed liberal arts junkie. He studied history at Yale, and got his graduate degree at Harvard where he studied ethics, religious studies and public policy. Herring's studies are relevant in business today. Core skills taught in the liberal arts like critical thinking, problem solving, and communications are in high demand today in every industry. "Hard skills" like math and science remain important too.[17]

In 1999 during the early days of online learning, Herring was employee number one at a learning technology research company called Lguide. They helped other companies make smart buying decisions about what was effective in asynchronous e-learning. The company eventually branched out into consulting and expanded their services to provide selective training outsourcing to large global corporations. In helping start Lguide, Herring learned about the training industry, what buyers were looking for, and the types of problems companies were trying to solve, such as cost reduction, speed, or talent engagement.

Around 2012, Herring sensed that the industry was changing and that people were starting to have different expectations around learning:

> *"I think the watershed moment from a technology perspective was around 2007 when the iPhone was launched, and YouTube was purchased by Google. A few years later, these technologies started showing up in the enterprise and employees were saying, 'Wow, I have these amazing experiences with my devices as a consumer, why am I putting up with this crap at work?'"*

So, Herring and his team saw an opportunity to do something different. They started testing a lot of new ideas, and he admits not all of them worked. It was an evolution; they started with some core ideas and then worked with some early customers whose input proved to be very influential in shaping their future product. They were also inspired by the MOOC concept being used in higher education, but they reimagined it in the context of work. Herring thought, "What if you could solve business problems with collaborative learning at scale versus just disseminating academic content?"

So, they put a question out there to some of their customers: Would they be interested in a learning platform that would help solve business problems? A platform that was highly scalable, highly engaging and collaborative, and involved group-driven learning experiences?

Herring says, "That sort of technology really didn't exist anywhere at that time. You had self-paced e-learning, webinar technology, and then higher education LMS technologies like Blackboard, but nothing that was really addressing the needs of corporate learning."

The question elicited a great response; people wanted to know what this sort of learning experience might look like. Within a year they had about a dozen customers who wanted to work with them, and that gave Herring and the team of 30 enough confidence to focus entirely on the collaborative learning technology. Eventually, in 2015, they sold the services side of the business to Xerox and launched Intrepid Learning as an independent technology business. In late 2017, following 750 percent growth and winning 40 industry awards in just three years, Intrepid was acquired by higher education leader VitalSource Technologies to lead VitalSource's corporate and professional learning technology business.

Intrepid was focused intently on enabling learner practice and real-world application of new skills on the job. "Too often learning and work are seen as two different worlds: it's a fatal flaw of event-based instructor-led training. While learners can get really engaged in a classroom experience, they often cannot directly apply new skills to actual work challenges in this environment, and they're certainly not doing much to reinforce these skills on the job." So Herring continued to focus on direct application of skills on the job and solving real work challenges, and wrapping learner collaboration around that. Intrepid does this by facilitating discussion forums, getting employees to engage in real work with their teams and reflect on what they are learning together, and helping individuals and teams learn over time.

The part about learning over time is important. Instead of trying to absorb a big data dump in an eight-hour classroom training session, our brains need time to process information. Learning over time gives us the opportunity to practice as well as to get reinforcements to our learning along the way.

Intrepid is a mission-driven company whose employees are most proud of enabling their customers and their partners to create transformative learning experiences for learners. The work they do goes beyond creating business impact; it impacts people's lives. Herring says, "Learning new skills really matters to people's ability to advance their careers. Whether mastering technical skills or core skills like communications and leadership, we have seen so many examples of people learning and applying a new skill that has helped them do their job better and move ahead at work. And at the same time, companies choose us to help them solve their stickiest, thorniest business and learning engagement challenges. At the end of the day, we are making a difference for people at work and the companies they work for, and that feels really good for all of us at Intrepid."

One of Intrepid's biggest success stories is its collaboration with Microsoft beginning in 2014[18] to create a new training approach for global sales teams. Microsoft had made the decision to evolve into a mobile-first cloud-first company—meaning a shift in focus from hardware and software to "cloud" products, such as servers, storage databases, business applications, more. But the transformation would have a significant impact on Microsoft's global sales teams. Rather than selling to IT managers, the global teams would be selling to business decision-makers typically operating in finance, accounting, and marketing departments, which required a very different sales approach.

The challenge facing Microsoft was clear: How could they train their global salesforce to adjust their sales technique to accommodate their new customer base?

Microsoft sales readiness leaders quickly realized the scope of the challenge. They knew it was a sea-change for the sales team, and as such it would require a new approach of significant magnitude. In response, Microsoft partnered with Intrepid to develop a "cloud mini-MBA" program with multiple business schools such as INSEAD, London Business School, Wharton and Kellogg to design collaborative, cohort-driven courses on Intrepid's technology platform. The programs included pre-recorded video lectures from professors, quizzes to test for understanding, online discussion forums, relevant case studies, and "mission" assignments (where participants created account plans for real customers).

Teams from all over the world were encouraged to communicate with each other, swap notes, and review each other's work. They were also able to track progress and compare that progress with their peers, an activity intended to spur friendly competition. At the end of each course, those who achieved the threshold percent pass rate and a passing grade on the real-world assignment received certificates from the relevant business school and a digital badge to use on their LinkedIn profile.

It's a great story because the outcomes were so valuable to Microsoft. Early on, when they measured the impact of the program, they showed it supported over $50 million in new revenue from just a couple hundred of the thousands of learners. And because team members created customer plans while taking the courses, field sales leadership was thrilled because account planning was a major priority for the team. In addition, the sales team loved the program. Individual engagement and satisfaction scores set new records for sales training programs at Microsoft. Not only did the outcomes show business impact and employee satisfaction, but also the program inspired some heartfelt testimonials from the sales reps, one of whom proudly announced, "I took this course, and because I took this course, I signed this deal with a bank for $25 million!"[19] Another employee was so impressed with the program that he spent twice the time recommended to follow it, just because he felt it was so beneficial to his career success and customer planning efforts.[20] With such great results, it is not surprising that Microsoft is continuing to use a custom MOOC training approach to teach a broad range of selling and core skills, and give teams from all over the world the chance to build relationships, share difficulties and insights, and communicate in a way that would never have been possible before.

Company Culture and Technology

New learning technologies require companies to change their mindset about their own learning and how they think about learning and work. Many companies are accustomed to command-and-control cultures, but in fact clarifying your company's fundamental philosophies is the key to success. For example, if a company buys technology that provides access to free learning content, but then blocks employees from accessing YouTube while they are at work, then the technology is at odds with the philosophy of the company. Similarly, if managers decide to track every piece of online content consumed by their employees and monitor how they complete their assignments, then that approach, too, flies in the face of giving employees ownership of their careers and learning journeys.

Companies need to adapt more to what their employees want and need. In addition, no technology is going to be a silver bullet. You can't just buy technology and expect that people will automatically convert. There will be work involved to make new technology successful—implementation, change management, executive buy-in, communication, and marketing all play a part in ongoing success.

Learning Technology Ecosystems

After figuring out why you want to do something with learning technology, chances are that you will want to do more than just one thing—you might want to help your employees discover their career goals or find their purpose. You might want to help them share their knowledge with peers; help them assess, learn, and build skills; and give them opportunities to practice their skills. Then you might discover that you can't find one company or one technology that does all these things—and maybe that's a good thing. At the onset, it may be more challenging to choose more than one technology. In the long run, though, companies should be thinking about creating a learning "ecosystem," which is a system that seamlessly integrates best-of-breed technologies for the problems that they want to solve.

There are other advantages of adopting a learning ecosystem philosophy. For example, if you are using a video content platform today and you've integrated it into your learning ecosystem, then later you find there is another video platform that suits your needs better, you can easily swap it out. You are not tied to every component of your ecosystem—it's ever evolving as technology continues to evolve too.

Many disruptive technologies in the market are changing the game when it comes to helping employees imagine their career goals, create and disseminate content, discover and consume information, and track skills and learning. There is something else unique about the number of forward-thinking, disruptive learning technologies emerging in the market: in most cases, the learning solutions are being created by people who are driven to make a difference in the world, whose mission is to scale technology to help people learn in unique and exciting ways.

Many of the education technology company founders such as those profiled in this chapter didn't create a technology solution just for the sake of making money. They created the solution because they were passionate about solving a particular business problem and saw a huge need that they could fill—and they wanted to have an impact in changing the way the world learns.

How to Create Your Learning Technology Ecosystem

For too long, businesses have stuck with the status quo, even when it's not working. But, there's also a balance. While you don't want to switch technologies constantly, you don't want to buy technology for problems you are not trying to solve, either. Here are some ways you can succeed with the right technology.

1. **Figure out your learning and talent strategy first.** It seems like common sense, but work out what you want to do, what your strategy is, and what business problems you are trying to solve before buying technology to support that strategy.
2. *Do your research.* There is plenty of great information out there about what technologies are available to solve your particular problems, so keep up to date on what's new. Some great resources for this include *Harvard Business Review* and *Fast Company.*
3. **Invest in adaptability more than efficiency.** Let go of the fantasy of one integrated system that does everything, all in a simple, seamless application. It feels familiar, it sounds safe, and it would be efficient. But locking all your processes, content, and users into one monolithic system won't help you adapt when requirements and priorities evolve, or when new, better options emerge. And they will.
4. **Focus on value, not price.** Look beyond the sticker price. According to Fosway Group's research, licensing fees account for only 35 percent of the total cost of "owning" company-wide software. Most of the expense actually comes after you sign, when you implement, operate, and innovate. So dig deeper. Consider productivity gains, think about new possibilities, and factor in the time and work it will take to drive adoption and utilization.
5. **Select a partner, not software.** Push past the sales rep. No matter how slick the user interface looks, or how easy the integrations sound, software won't transform your operations or make

change stick. People will. Innovation takes vision, creativity, and grit, but it also requires solving problems. So get to know the product as well as the engineering and client service people you'll be working with. Your success depends on their flexibility, experience, and skills, too.

When General Mills' former talent development leader Susie McNamara evaluates new technologies for learning, she scrutinizes more than the technology itself. "I not only look at what the technology does and the experience that it's creating," she says, "but I also think about the entire package. What do I get when I buy this? Do I get a team of curators? Do I get a marketing team? Those answers have made my decisions for me in a lot of cases. I'm not just buying a technology or a product. I'm buying an entire team of people. I see them as an extension of my team."[21]

CHAPTER SEVEN

Analyze Skills with Data and Insights

RECENTLY, KELLY HAD a conversation with the head of sales in one of the biggest tech companies in Silicon Valley. He wanted to know what his salespeople were learning, the skills they already had, and what they needed to do to close more deals. The bottom line was that he wanted his sales reps to make their quota so he could make his numbers. He wanted to help his company succeed and get the most out of his team. He also wanted to move his organization ahead of the curve and understand the learning and skills his salespeople needed for the future to continue to hit their numbers.

When he asked his team for help with his challenges and questions, he got a 50-page report with return-on-investment (ROI) calculations on learning programs that he didn't believe—and that was painful to slog through. In his frustration, he threw the report in the garbage. It didn't tell him what he wanted to know. Business leaders and CEOs face this predicament all the time: not getting the information they need about how learning makes teams more successful.

Maybe you have been in this sales leader's position, where you have received complex calculations attempting to show the correlation or causation of how training impacts business results. Most likely you have been asked to fill out surveys—commonly called "smiley sheets"—that ask how you like a particular training class, but that in reality tell you only how people liked the instructor or the experience during an event. The most common and useless metric is totaling the number of hours and people who actually sit in a class, which tells you nothing. Think about it—if someone tells you that 36 of your salespeople completed an online ethics training course and 45 completed a class on sales methodology, what are you supposed to do with that information? That data doesn't provide any valuable insight, but that's the data most leaders get in companies today. It doesn't tell the story business leaders and CEOs need to hear. Part of the problem is that generally we don't understand employees' skills gaps, and it's difficult to measure what people actually learn. On top of that, it's nearly impossible to correlate learning to the company's success. Overall, leaders don't even have a baseline to understand the skills of their teams, and so far, nothing has enlightened them. Yet things are changing.

As David often says, "The market wants to speak the language of skills, but we haven't had a good way to do that until now." With the help of data and analytics, we have the ability to understand our employees' current skills as well as the ones they are building. Data can also tell us the level of engagement in learning, how to make the best learning investment decisions, and how learning can impact the business in significant ways. Thanks to personalization and technology, we now have the capability to access a tremendous amount of data regarding how people learn, what people learn, and how it affects their work. If we analyze the data, we can gain insights and use predictive analytics to look forward rather than always looking back.

Data can answer some of the critical questions leaders ask about training, such as:

- Should we be spending this much money to train our employees?
- Is it making a difference?
- Was it worth the investment?
- What are employees learning on their own time and on the job that we aren't tracking?

In our Degreed research, we found that across 150 companies and over three million users, 68 percent of the content people consumed came not from their company's LMS or other company sources. Instead it came from employees' self-directed learning of all of the free, informal content that is available. More than two decades ago, Peter Senge wrote in his book *The Fifth Discipline*, "The only sustainable competitive advantage is an organization's ability to learn faster than the competition."[1] While that still holds true, the data we use to show how, what, and when our employees learn is better than ever. If all leaders had this data at their fingertips, they might make different investment decisions about learning for their employees.

Corporate Learning as a Business

To further understand the value of data when it comes to learning strategy, it's important to look at how some of the most successful companies think about corporate learning. Since corporate learning is often viewed as a cost center rather than a revenue-generating function, learning typically becomes more reactive than strategic. For example, one business leader asks for a conscious bias training program, another wants an agile development training program, and maybe a third asks for an onboarding program. So here are three discreet learning programs, but no larger learning strategy to frame what the business is trying to accomplish. A strong learning leader who understands business can develop an overall learning strategy based on data from several sources and show how this learning can impact both the business and employees in meaningful ways.

Many successful learning leaders do not start out in the learning field. Instead, they often come from marketing, product development, product management, technology, and corporate strategy. These leaders can take advantage of their business background to approach learning more as a business than as a support function or service and apply the principles of business to make learning a strategic competitive advantage.

Janice Burns, chief learning officer at MasterCard, is a good example of a successful learning leader who comes from a business background. Before making the move into learning, she spent time in MasterCard's product, marketing, and customer satisfaction organizations. Similarly, Heather Kirkby moved from key roles in product management and marketing at Intuit to become vice president of Intuit's talent development function. Beth Galetti, senior vice president of HR at Amazon, was originally CIO at FedEx before taking over the HR and learning function at Amazon. Finally, Tim Quinlan at Intel worked in sales, marketing, and technology before leading Intel's digital learning strategy.

Susie Lee,[2] head of global business solutions at Degreed, is another leader who started in business before moving to learning. In 2010, Lee moved internally from her role at Bank of America as vice president of product development and loyalty marketing to senior vice president of global learning product management and implementations.

When Lee first joined corporate learning, the organization was mired in process and order taking. It was very reactive and event driven. It was difficult to get data. Without good data it was impossible to analyze what was working and what wasn't, or to even determine the type of metrics to analyze.

Lee noticed that by applying the principles of marketing and metrics to corporate learning, she was able to engage in meaningful conversations with business leaders about the learning patterns of employees.

Lee believes one of the smartest things companies can do is look at corporate learning more holistically and think of learning as a business. In the simplest form, that means understanding your customers. But who are your learning customers in a corporation? Often learning organizations think that their customers are the executives who are asking for the training for their teams. Or they think their customers are in the HR organization, since they are also asking for training programs, assuming they know what's best for the employees. But, ultimately (and this is where the shift in mindset is important), the customers are your employees. They are the ones who are doing the learning. That's why it's even more important to focus on learning data to give you insights about what skills your employees have and what learning they need to get the skills they need. Then, it's not about guesswork; instead, it's about data showing what employees really need. This also happens in businesses where engineers think they know what the customer wants, but they haven't actually ever talked to one of their customers. In learning, you need to look at data from your employees so that you know where the business is succeeding, or where you may need to make changes.

When learning programs or learning technologies are viewed as products rather than events, then strategy, marketing, and success metrics become second nature. According to Lee, you can use data in layers: first look at metrics and data at the product level, then at the program level, and then at the course level. Once you have data at those levels, you can use qualitative and quantitative measurement strategies to get insights that enable you to pivot and change what's happening in the business and become more outcome driven.[3]

For example, say you have several content libraries in your learning ecosystem, and you've discovered through data that no one is accessing or engaging with one particular learning library—which costs your business about $300,000 a year. Armed with this information, you could make the case through data insights to either divest in this learning product, to invest in different content, or to realize overall cost savings.

In another example, imagine your company has developed a learning program for building management skills, but your qualitative and quantitative research or data tells you the program or product is not making a difference. Just like if you are marketing a product, you would get customer input and make changes based on that input to get the results that you want. Customer feedback as one data point provides valuable insights for companies and indicates what you need to change and how you need to pivot the business to motivate and change your employees' behavior.

Lee added, "Too often internal technology projects, when not managed as a product or run like a business, are influenced by people's opinions instead of reality." For example, at one large corporation there was an initiative to invest in refreshing dozens of SharePoint sites for learning when the data indicated that the usage was really low. "If you make the case with data, it is a pretty straightforward business decision that you wouldn't spend the money—the SharePoint sites aren't being used so don't invest to recreate them."[4]

Measuring What Matters with the Learning Analytics Model

As Lee discovered, data insights enabled her to have meaningful conversations with leaders about the impact of employee learning. The smartest companies succeed using data and insights to tell a compelling story. Many companies apply the principles of the learning analytics model (LAM) to acquire information. This model shows you how to:

- Collect the right learning data
- Analyze that data to find powerful insights
- Tell a compelling story about learning at your company to help gain a competitive advantage
- Provide actionable outcomes using this data

The model provides business outcomes based on those insights, which may lead to actions or recommendations to either change or further develop the learning process.

Once you collect all the relevant data, it's time for analysis. The goal of analyzing the learning data is to help you figure out what it all means and get the answers you're looking for. Analyzing data is part science and part art, and it is one of the most in-demand skills in business today having grown over 650 percent since 2012.[5] Overall, being able to analyze data will become more important for everyone moving forward.

Data can be collected at a variety of levels to tell a complete learning story. For example, you can collect data at the industry level, the company level, the organizational level, and the individual (employee) level. There are several inputs across each of these levels that you can use to help tell the learning story:

Industry Level

What are the most needed skills in the industry? What are the skills of our competitors, and how do we match up? Collect data through industry benchmark studies and analyst reports. For example, say you are a growing cybersecurity company and you discover through a Cybersecurity Ventures report that jobs are in high demand, and they predict there will be 3.5 million unfilled cybersecurity positions by 2021. That would inform your business strategy and how you will need to compete for talent in the future.

Company Level

What are the most important strategic drivers and metrics in the business? For example, say your customers' requests for expertise on data insights keeps growing. So, to stay competitive, you've taken that input and decided to invest in data experts by planning to hire or develop 5,000 data scientists during the next five years.

Organizational/Team Level

What skills do your people have and what skills do your people need to stay competitive? Collect data through assessments (skill self-assessments, 360 assessments, peer assessments, manager assessments), feedback, learning goals, adaptive learning, and voice-of-the-customer. For example, suppose you lead a product management team at your company, and you discover through self-assessments and manager assessments that prioritization is a critical skill for your product managers. If some of your team members are not strong in that skill and you think it's important, you can provide feedback to those employees so they can focus on that skill as a learning goal.

Individual Level

How and what are your employees learning? What skills do they have and need to build? Collect data about both formal and informal learning as well as skills gaps through research, surveys, learning technology platform analytics, Google Analytics, machine learning data, and voice-of-the-customer. Just knowing what people are learning and what skills they are building can be incredibly powerful. At Degreed, we track this data regularly using our own product to see what skills we have within the organization. Then, when there is an internal opening that requires those skills, we have a good idea who is interested because we have the data. Employees are excited when they see opportunities tied to the new learning and skills they are developing.

Analyze Data: Industry Level

At the industry level, you can look at data a few different ways. Let's take as an example the World Economic Forum 2018 *The Future of Jobs* report,[6] which highlights skills disruption data by country and industry. The report states that 35 percent of core skills will be disrupted in the work-force between 2015 and 2020, as illustrated in figure 7.1. It also indicates that around the world, 210 million people will change their occupation by 2030.

Figure 7.1[7] The Future of Jobs Report, World Economic Forum 2018

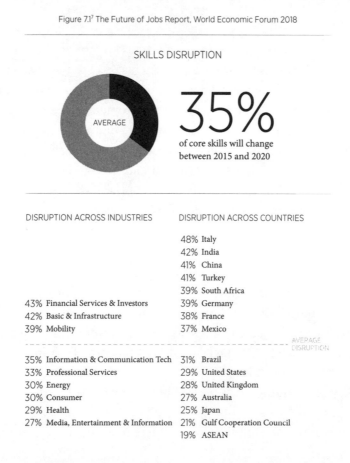

SKILLS DISRUPTION

AVERAGE

35%
of core skills will change
between 2015 and 2020

DISRUPTION ACROSS INDUSTRIES

DISRUPTION ACROSS COUNTRIES

	48% Italy
	42% India
	41% China
	41% Turkey
	39% South Africa
43% Financial Services & Investors	39% Germany
42% Basic & Infrastructure	38% France
39% Mobility	37% Mexico

AVERAGE
DISRUPTION

35% Information & Communication Tech	31% Brazil
33% Professional Services	29% United States
30% Energy	28% United Kingdom
30% Consumer	27% Australia
29% Health	25% Japan
27% Media, Entertainment & Information	21% Gulf Cooperation Council
	19% ASEAN

So how can you analyze this data to connect with your own data? First, look at what's happening across similar companies in your industry, and then look at data across geographies. For example, if you are in the financial services industry in Italy, the data shows 43 percent skills disruption in your industry, and 48 percent skills disruption in your country. Those are two important data points to include in your analysis of how your organization measures up in terms of skills.

According to Maksim Ovsyannikov, former vice president of product at Degreed, "Skills are not only becoming the currency of learning, but also an economic indicator, and the very language of workforce analytics."[8] Figure 7.2 illustrates the contrast between the most abundant skills in the San Francisco Bay Area compared to the most scarce skills.

Figure 7.2[9] Most Abundant and Scarce Skills in the San Francisco Bay Area

January 2018	January 2018
MOST ABUNDANT SKILLS IN THE SAN FRANCISCO BAY AREA	**MOST SCARCE SKILLS IN THE SAN FRANCISCO BAY AREA**
1. Perl/Python/Ruby	1. Healthcare Management
2. Cloud and Distributed Computing	2. Sales
3. Integrated Circuit (IC) Design	3. Education and Teaching
4. C/C++	4. Purchasing and Contract Navigation
5. Mobile Development	5. Microsoft Windows Systems
6. Other Software Development Skills	6. Retail Store Operations
7. Java Development	7. IT Infrastructure & System Mgmt
8. Scripting Languages	8. General Finance
9. Web Programming	9. Marketing Event Management
10. Software and User Testing	10. Other HR

The data in figure 7.2 from LinkedIn shows there is an abundance of software developers in the San Francisco Bay Area, and that in fact the top 10 skills are all technology related. Then, if you look at the skills gaps, the data shows that we need more people with healthcare and sales skills as well as education and marketing skills. So, if you are an employer, you might realize that it's going to be tougher to recruit for those skills that are most scarce. If you are an individual, you may be excited to see that if you learn skills in marketing event management, there are job opportunities in San Francisco for people with those skills. Overall, the goal is to collect as much industry data as possible from a variety of sources to identify patterns in your own organization.

Analyze Data: Company Level

When analyzing data at the company level, it helps to get a good sense of how learning is impacting your company overall. Metrics like productivity, job effectiveness, and internal career progression provide a greater insight into how learning influences your company. If one of your company's goals is to make learning a competitive advantage by attracting new talent or keeping the great talent you already have, this data will help you tell a compelling story.

In August 2017, Janice Burns,[10] MasterCard's chief learning officer, conducted an impact study involving around 1,000 MasterCard employees to gather data for analysis at the company level. The data indicated that active users of MasterCard's new learning platform were more likely to say they're more productive (54 percent), more effective in their job or role (51 percent), and more invested in growing their careers (46 percent) than non-users. Burns was also able to tell from the data that active users were 33 percent more likely to say they're engaged at work than non-users, and 80 percent more likely to say they're more collaborative. These metrics reflect the progress and feedback directly from Master-Card learners. This is the kind of data that can help tell the learning story at a company level.

Again, this data points to insights that are valuable in developing an overall talent strategy. Burns uses these metrics on an ongoing basis to inform her talent strategy. This is an agile way for her to respond to any changes initiated by employees, as it enables her to adjust the tactics in her strategy.

Analyze Data: Organizational/Team Level

Analyzing data at the organizational level involves looking for patterns across similar job functions. The goal here is to narrow your focus on data that will be interesting not only to the company, but specifically to business leaders across different departments, such as the head of engineering or the head of sales. For example, if you analyze data from the engineering organization, it helps that leader design a talent strategy for engineers, which will probably differ from the talent strategy designed for salespeople.

Figure 7.3 shows an organizational-level view of data for a specific function, in this case the corporate learning function. This data provides leaders of learning organizations with information about the types of skills their employees already have as well as the ones they will need for the future.

The organizational level involves looking at trends and patterns in a funnel, first starting with macro data and then narrowing that focus to your team or organization. For example, when it comes to your learning team, the data might show that you have a high number of project managers and instructional designers, but very few technologists or data analysts. This data provides you with intelligence on the skills your team has versus the skills your team needs.

When applied to an engineering team, the data may show that 80 percent of your developers are web developers, but that only 20 percent have mobile development skills. If your company strategy is moving toward mobile, then you now have the data that tells you the mix needs to change. This is a valuable insight for business leaders who are planning their business and talent strategy for the future.

Figure 7.3[11] Top L&D Skills That Organizations Have And Want

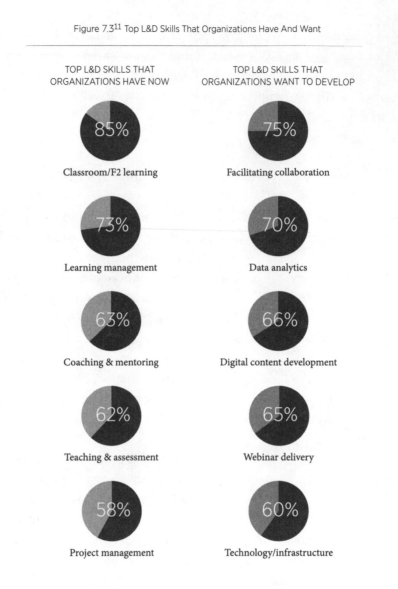

TOP L&D SKILLS THAT
ORGANIZATIONS HAVE NOW

TOP L&D SKILLS THAT
ORGANIZATIONS WANT TO DEVELOP

85%
Classroom/F2 learning

75%
Facilitating collaboration

73%
Learning management

70%
Data analytics

63%
Coaching & mentoring

66%
Digital content development

62%
Teaching & assessment

65%
Webinar delivery

58%
Project management

60%
Technology/infrastructure

At the team level, it's essential that you know the skills your people already have. It's amazing that most leaders don't have this insight beyond what their employees are hired to do. When Kelly was leading the learning function at LinkedIn, she wanted to develop a brand for the organization, and design marketing campaigns for their learning products. As it happened, there was a person in Kelly's organization, Nawal Fakhoury, who had a degree in Public Relations as well as experience creating a brand for learning products at a prior company. Kelly only became aware of this skill set during a conversation, since Nawal had been hired to lead onboarding for LinkedIn. In this case, Nawal was thrilled to consult on this initiative and provide her skills and expertise to the team.

If there was a good way to know all the skills of the people in your team or organization, it would be much easier to give your talent new opportunities to grow and develop.

Analyze Data: Individual Level

Data at the individual level enables you to gain a clear picture of the type of learning your employees are engaged in. In the past, it was possible to gain insight into only a fraction of what people were learning. Thanks to new learning technology, it is now easier to obtain data on learning both formally and informally, inside and outside your company. The goal of analyzing data at the individual level is to use the data to tell the story of the type of content being consumed by employees, as well as what they are learning.

In 2017, Degreed began work with NASA's Jet Propulsion Laboratory (JPL). JPL is a unique national research facility that carries out robotic space and Earth science missions. According to Tony Gagliardo, the company's head of learning, JPL is responsible for sending astronauts to the moon and also manages NASA's Deep Space Network, a worldwide system of antennas that communicates with interplanetary spacecraft. It has some of the world's most advanced technology and brightest minds, but even these rocket scientists need to be continually learning. Gagliardo said, "We recognize the shift is already under way in the technology, skills, and employee demographic that will lead us into the future, so we needed to shift our learning strategy and technology ecosystem as well."[12]

They wanted to understand what their scientists were learning to remain innovative and up-to-date on the latest technologies. To do that, they had to collect meaningful data about what their employees were doing and figure out ways to measure learning and skills.

Let's look at some answers to the questions posed by JPL. First: *Are people learning?* One of the most important attributes people can have, regardless of where they work, is learning agility and the desire to continuously learn. When you are looking at data you've gathered, take time to focus on the level of learning engagement. Can you measure whether people in your company are actually engaged in learning? Are they accessing the content and the systems that you've put in place for learning? If so, how often do they engage? Analyzing data based on weekly active users, monthly active users, activations, or logins to learning systems is one way to set a baseline engagement metric.

Second: *How are people learning?* Are they learning from going to conferences, reading books, or recommending content to peers? Are they involved in team learning programs or projects? The insights here can help you understand where you can make smart learning investments and where you might need to make some changes. For example, if the data tells you that all your engineers are learning from Pluralsight's content library, but your company only offers content from Lynda.com, you may want to change the investment portfolio for learning. Or, you may find that your employees are learning from such a wide variety of sources that it makes more sense to allocate money per employee to learn what they want, and then track it. That way you can continue to collect data to help you understand how they are learning.

The final two questions are: *What skills do people have?* and *What skills do they need?* Understanding what skills your people have versus what skills people need is critically important for companies analyzing their talent. Companies need to know if they have people with the skills that will take them into the future. For example, a few years ago in the engineering organization at Yahoo!, there was a struggle to find mobile developers because tech companies were snapping up as many as they could hire. It resulted in a scramble to develop the engineers that they had, because hiring had become so difficult. If you could predict the type of skills your engineers would need for the future, you could start to help them develop those skills early rather than try to compete for talent with other companies later.

Wrong Data Can Be Deadly

However, even with all that data at hand, we do have to be a bit cautious since showing wrong data can be deadly. At a tech company Kelly worked at, the HR team came into a business review with some data about the talent in their company. Immediately, the VP of engineering said, "Those numbers aren't right for my organization." Once that comment was out there, other executives began to question the data about their organization as well. Dani Johnson, former analyst with Bersin by Deloitte, says, "Data can either build credibility or it can kill it. We need to understand how [learning] efforts are affecting performance, and we should be able to speak to it and adapt as necessary. If everyone else is talking about product throughput or turnover and we are talking about learner satisfaction, there is disconnect."[13] Especially for data-driven leaders, if someone can point out errors in the data you show, you won't get to tell the story behind the data. It just won't be credible.

Janice Burns, chief learning officer at MasterCard, believes we are still on a journey with learning analytics. She suggests that "we can make some progress by building a robust technology ecosystem to bring fragmented learning data together." Burns notes that some of the issues with data analytics are still being uncovered and that privacy laws and the fact that more and more questions are being asked about how we use the data could be one challenge.

But data is going to be key moving forward. She said, "You not only need a learning strategy, but a data strategy and technology strategy as well. And to get insights you need other types of data—not only learning data, but talent data and acquisition data. The key is to tell a story and pull it all together."

Telling the Learning Story at Your Company

So why would you want to hear the learning story at your company? If you are used to seeing reports of who completed the ethics compliance training last month, it's a snooze. You can't really be expected to care and, frankly, most companies only care about who took compliance training when a lawsuit comes around.

But, if you look at learning in a different way—as a way to understand the most competent person to assign to a particular project, or as a means of finding out which team members are actively learning the new skills really needed by your organization—the learning becomes a powerful part of your talent and business strategy.

Even better, with the help of the right data, you can tell a compelling learning story rather than just provide a spreadsheet of endless data. Stories are a great way to engage an audience. They provide a vehicle to transmit impactful messages. According to leadership consultant Kristi Hedges, "Stories grab us. They take us in, transport us, and allow us to live vicariously and visually through another's experience." In addition, "Shared stories accelerate interpersonal connection. Learning to tell stories to capture, direct, and sustain the attention of others is a key leadership skill."[14] Storytelling can be a compelling way to tell the learning story and really share your understanding of the degree of talent in your organization.

CHAPTER EIGHT

Make Expertise Count

IF YOU WERE to ask someone about their health and they told you that they ran a marathon 20 years ago, what would you think? Similarly, when someone asks you, "Tell me about your education," how do you answer? Most of us immediately think about our formal education—the degrees or certificates we have earned. You might mention the university, college, or school you graduated from. Or you'll respond that you didn't go to college, or you haven't finished your degree. Whether you're 20 years into your career or 20 months, you'll answer the question about your education through the lens of formal schooling.

Which is absurd.

Does your answer tell the story of all the learning you've done? Does it capture all the knowledge and experience—both formal and informal—you have accumulated since you graduated?

Of course not.

You don't stop learning once you finish school. We learn the entirety of our lives, everywhere we go. But most of the time you are likely not very intentional about what you learn and how you acquire new knowledge. Instead, learning happens in an organic way: you learn a new skill by watching a peer give a presentation, or because you picked up a book or stumbled onto a TED Talk. In the expertise economy, it's not important how you gain your expertise, just that you did. The challenge we are left with is how we make expertise count in meaningful ways, so we can use it to secure jobs, advance careers, and change the world.

We are all trying to keep up with what we need to learn. Accelerations in technology and science are outpacing the capacity of humans and society to adapt. While new methods are making old methods obsolete, adapting slowly is no longer sufficient. Pulitzer Prize–winning journalist and author Thomas L. Friedman writes about this concept in *Thank You for Being Late: An Optimist's Guide to Thriving in the Age of Accelerations*.[1] According to Friedman, our educational system is outdated: there are a million people around the world who can do our job, and because of this, we all need to engage in a lifelong learning process to acquire new expertise if we want to thrive in the workplace. Although countries, governments, CEOs, business leaders, and employees are beginning to feel the rate of acceleration and disruption, we are already behind.[2]

The problem is that the currency of our skills today is determined by the measure of a college degree, rather than by what you know or can do presently. In the United States, more people have college degrees than ever before.[3] Today 33.4 percent of Americans have completed a bachelor's degree or higher compared with 1940, when that number was just 4.6 percent.

Yet if someone attends university for just three years and does not complete the four-year degree, they don't get credit for learning anything. Even if they do complete the four-year degree, does that really tell the story about what a person can do? Does it represent all the skills and expertise a person has gained over their working life? Recall David's conversation with a woman who was 30 years beyond when she would have attended college. When he asked her, "Tell me about your education," she considered herself to be uneducated because she didn't have a formal degree. That's a travesty.

The fact is that—with or without a degree—many of today's employees are gaining skills and knowledge all the time. Furthermore, they actively want to quantify their skills. For instance, a skills and expertise survey conducted by team-building platform TeamFit[4] shows that employees want to invest the time and effort to understand their own skills and their potential for their careers. The survey also shows that senior leaders and managers want to understand their employees' skills to put people into the right roles—or, even more importantly—to put their employees in a position to help their companies solve the most critical problems in their industry.

Skills for a Nation

Being able to understand the expertise economy on a holistic basis—your country's skills, your industry's skills, your company's skills, as well as the skills you have as an individual—is the currency of the future. The SkillsFuture program[5] is a great example of a countrywide initiative to emphasize the value of skills. Launched in 2015 by the Singaporean government, the initiative provides all citizens with access to training programs to develop specific skills. The mission of the program is to create a rich talent pool of the most in-demand skills and provide a platform where workers can develop and display their expertise. By working in partnership with employers, unions, and professional bodies, the government acts as both an education provider and a broker to enable newly skilled labor to find work related to their skills.

The program also includes career and skill development programs for domains ranging from the energy sector, engineering and software development, aerospace, food service, finance, and many other skilled fields. The development and measurement of these skills is the secret sauce that unlocks the mobility of the workforce. In 2017, more than 285,000 people benefited from these training programs in Singapore.

Building Relevant Skills for a Company

Traditionally, CEOs have focused an inordinate amount of their time on company profit and loss. Increasingly, though, they are focusing on talent and education, realizing the impact on their company's overall business strategy. At a recent Fortune magazine-sponsored event for CEOs on corporate brand-building, two of the key topics were "Closing the Skills Gap: Unlocking Opportunity in Workforce Development" and

"The CEO's New Imperative: How Corporate Culture Drives Innovation and Lasting Business Success."

Business leaders are embracing the idea that it's critical to have a skill-based business strategy for their company and that culture is integral in that strategy. The trend we're seeing is that the most forward-thinking CEOs are prioritizing and taking ownership of learning as part of their company strategy. They are speaking publicly about the importance of learning and education in the workforce in general, and for their own employees specifically. It's a key differentiator in recruiting and keeping the best talent.

So how are company CEOs tackling the big task of building relevant skills for their companies and employees? Bill McDermott, CEO of SAP, thinks that it's never too late to learn. He's looking at the issue from the view of the maturing workforce as well as the new college grads entering the workforce. Fundamentally, McDermott believes that age is irrelevant, and you are never too old (or young) to develop new skills and learn.[6]

McDermott recalled a story he heard from the Prime Minister of Japan about an 81-year-old woman who developed a software application while at a nursing home and it was so good, she started her own business. McDermott believes that "It's never too late to retool, retrain, and get yourself focused on something new." He applies this belief to the employees at SAP, many of whom have been with the company since its inception and are among his most valuable employees. He says that even if you are a new college grad, technical or IT skills are not the most important skills to have. McDermott believes soft skills and emotional intelligence are incredibly important. "What you need is empathy. The idea of being in service to other people is the greatest form of leadership." When SAP is recruiting new talent, they look for a person's desire to learn and a natural proclivity to do something well first, and then try to match the hard skills of the prospective employee with the opportunity.

McDermott believes strongly in developing his employees at SAP, "We started an academy. We hire our own, we train our own, we build our own." What really stands out about McDermott's leadership in helping his employees build skills, is that at most companies, training is consistently the first budget item to be cut. But for SAP, McDermott says "The one line-item in the budget that no manager in the company can cut is training because we believe that education is the key to every-thing." For employees to hear their CEO say that is not only powerful, it's a game changer.

Boeing is also making a big bet on employee learning. This year they announced they are investing $100 million in their employees' learning and skills. They took an interesting approach to their initiative and actu-ally crowdsourced more than 40,000 ideas from their employees world-wide. What their employees told them was that they wanted learning that was accessible to all employees at the company and that every person at every level needs to build skills for the future.[7]

According to Heidi Capozzi, Senior Vice President at Boeing, "we listened and read every single idea that was submitted. Our long-term plans represent a down payment on the future of our employees and tomorrow's technical workforce." Boeing will focus on programs that help employees grow and build technical skills, understand industry trends, and learn new tools and technologies.[8]

Boeing plans to launch a wide variety of workforce development programs and are partnering with Degreed to provide access to online learning and education, certification courses, and degree programs. As a huge enabler of Boeing's growth strategies, they will first offer a pro-gram that focuses on digital literacy. It's impressive the number of edu-cation and career growth initiatives Boeing offers including internships, boot camps, rotational programs, formal mentorships, and leadership training—the $100 million investment is above and beyond those pro-grams they were already offering.

If you think company strategies focused on building employee skills are just for CEOs of technology companies, think again. Drew Green-blatt is the CEO of manufacturing company Marlin Steel Wire Products and he's known the power of having as many employees as possible cross-trained in as many skills as possible for years. It's given his com-pany the flexibility required to respond to the constant changes at work and in the world. He's evolved the company from one that makes wire baskets for bagel retailers to a fast-growing manufacturer of specialty precision metal fabrications used by auto companies like Toyota and multi-national defense contractors like BAE.[9]

Greenblatt has made a huge investment in the skills of his front-line employees providing them with the tools, training, and incentives that help them earn a strong middle-class living. Instead of competing on price, driving down wages, and offering fewer benefits, Greenblatt values his people and invests in their skills, motivates them, and then compensates them based on the new skills they learn and the proficiency that they've achieved in those skills. What he's gotten in return are loyal employees who are learning how to operate computer-controlled routers, presses, and robots that have taken over some of the automated tasks.

Greenblatt is ahead of his time. While some are just starting to think about how humans and machines will co-exist in the workforce, he's been doing it for years. His forward-thinking approach to investing in his people is not really new. According to Steven Pearlstein who interviewed Greenblatt recently, the principles Greenblatt follows come from business books published decades ago. But, for some reason, companies have forgotten some of the important business management principles. Greenblatt's philosophy is "they do well, we do well; we do well, they do well. That's the deal."[10]

Individuals Focusing on Skilling and Reskilling

Of course, not everybody needs to work for a big organization to acquire the skills they need. Take Mikel Blake,[11] for example. Blake grew up in a very traditional culture in Utah. She graduated from Brigham Young University (BYU) in 2006 with a degree in International Relations. She met her husband, David, the cofounder of Degreed, in college, and they decided to get married and start a family. While Blake was studying for the LSAT, David was interviewing at consulting firms across the country. David landed a management consulting job in Dallas, so Blake decided to put her lawyer ambitions on hold, and, after having her first child, she decided to stay at home to raise their family.

A few years later, a new job opportunity for David took them back to Utah and close to BYU. During the summer term, Blake, still feeling a career calling, decided to audit a computer science course. A professor at BYU agreed to allow her to sit in the class for the term, which fueled Blake's interest in the topic. She enthusiastically completed all the assignments and homework and really enjoyed the experience, but she didn't pursue it further at that time. Eventually, she and David ended up moving to San Francisco with their two small children.

Nearly 10 years after she got her degree at BYU, Blake realized that she wanted to continue to raise her family, but that she also wanted to pursue a career—she wanted to work and realize her full professional potential. But what did this mean? Pursuing law school? Computer science? Or getting a part-time job just to keep her busy? After much soul searching, Blake realized what she really wanted was a career. Yet she felt conflicted between working and being a stay-at-home mom. After a lot of deliberation, she finally came to the realization that her family would all benefit from her pursuing her passions to find a fulfilling career.

In 2012, Blake discovered Codecademy, an online, interactive platform that provides free online tutorials and classes. Through this platform, she was able to learn to code interactively in the evenings after her kids went to bed. She took another year off from coding when she gave birth to her third child. When she was ready to start again, she felt, given her limited hours, that she had gone as far as she could on her own, and once again, went online for some inspiration. There she came across a group based in San Francisco called MotherCoders whose mission was "To help women with kids on-ramp to careers in tech so they can thrive in the digital economy."[12] That program really helped Blake become oriented to the tech world and all the different options available. When she completed the program, she felt incredibly energized to keep going.

Eventually, Blake enrolled in a full-time development boot camp called Dev Mountain. Over the course of three months' full-time study, she learned software development to prepare her for a coding job in tech. However, the course didn't guarantee a job at the end of it—after all, it was only three months; not only would she be competing with her fellow boot camp participants, but also with people who had four-year computer science degrees.

Once Blake completed the boot camp, she took an internship for a year, coding real projects, which proved to be invaluable experience.

Thanks to her mentors and the variety of projects she was assigned to work on, she was able to figure out which area of software development she actually wanted to focus on. Not long after the internship, she was hired on as a contractor and then a full-time position as a web developer.

Blake's career journey is both inspirational and relatively atypical. Ultimately, she took a very untraditional path with many starts and stops to develop her expertise and build her career as a web developer. Through her years of learning, Blake found that she could have a fulfilling career and raise a family. She also proved to be a great model for owning your own learning and career.

Hiring Practices: From Traditional to Skills-Based

Whether it's building skills for citizens of a nation like Singapore, helping employees build new and emerging skills within a company like Boeing or SAP, or reskilling yourself to pursue a new career like Mikel Blake, it's not easy to talk about skills as a currency because there is no standard language around skills.

This is because traditional hiring practices don't recognize skills as the key to recruiting and building internal and external talent.

For instance, imagine you're hiring for an open position inside your organization. What parameters do you use to make a hiring decision? Chances are you base it solely on a person's qualifications. Assume you have a great pool of applicants. How do you winnow the field down to just a few? Which person ultimately receives an offer?

Quite possibly you have technology that sorts resumés, cover letters, or LinkedIn profiles for certain keywords and phrases. These tools are designed to narrow down the mass of online job applications. After initial filtering, you are left with a couple dozen applications, which are maybe reviewed by an internal team or person, who then selects several of the applicants for initial screening interviews. That process narrows the field to three or four. One or two applications go through the full series of interviews, and ultimately an offer is sent out.

When we hire people, from within a company or externally, the question we should be answering is *Can this person do the job and how well?* In other words, we should be assessing people's abilities through the lens of skills rather than more conflated signals like the company a person worked for or a prestigious school they attended. Skills are the things we can do. Mastery is how well we can do them. Can she program in Python? Can he think critically? Can she present? Can he analyze? If so, how well? Every job we ask someone to do is a compilation of individual skills. Skills are the building blocks of a job, and the building blocks of a company. When we analyze our talent—both internally and externally—we should be looking at the skills people have and how well they have mastered those skills.

Instead, we tend to use the following proxies for skills in the labor market:

Job titles

The problem with using job titles as signals of expertise and skill is that they are not ubiquitous. The meaning behind a job title varies greatly from one company, industry, or geography to another. When considering job titles, think about the skills you think a director has that a manager does not. Are those correct assumptions?

Pedigree of university

Granted, where a person went to college often creates a certain impression—intelligence, perhaps, a specific set of values, a sense of stick-to-it-ness. It can also indicate the type of training a person has received. But hiring decisions cannot be based on where someone went to school because, overall, it tells you little about the candidate's current portfolio of skills.

Logos on a resumé

"Wow, this person worked at Google; he must be amazing!" Well, maybe, but maybe not. Logos on resumés give no indication of what people can do and how well they can do it.

References

Character references are a good thing, but it is important not to conflate positive references with skills. A reference may be great when it comes to validating a candidate's work ethic or honesty, but it's not the best way to prove the degree of financial planning and analysis skills (FP&A) or critical-thinking abilities.

Interviewing skills

While interviews are essential to the hiring process, they don't tell you everything about a candidate. For example, some people interview very well, only to founder once the job is theirs. Don't confuse magnanimity with ability.

GPA/SAT/ACT

Believe it or not, some companies still use GPA, or scores on standardized exams, as signals of expertise or potential inside a company. These measures were never meant to signal expertise, and so they also fall into the bucket of proxy measures for the thing we care about. In other words, just because you score well on a test doesn't mean you can successfully do a job.

For us to solve the labor market problems we have in this economy, we must begin speaking the language of skills and stop caring about pedigrees, logos, time spent learning, test-taking ability, interviewing skills, or anything else. The first step to speaking this language is to think of your company as its own labor market.

Your Company Is a Labor Market

While your organization is part of the labor market at large, it's also a microcosm of the labor market. You have a labor pool, with open positions to be filled, in which you recruit, fire, promote, analyze, and assess your talent. The labor market is made of a supply side and a demand side. The supply side is comprised of the workers and those who prepare those workers for the labor market, including higher education establishments, professional associations, apprentice programs, boot camps and so on. The demand side of the labor market is the jobs to be done to help you achieve your organizational goals. In addition to companies, there are also brokers, job boards, recruiters, and influential people that match people to opportunities.

The big advantage companies have is that it's a completely vertically integrated market—you own the entire process—and so you can drive a level of efficiency that the overall labor market would be very hard pressed to match.

Creating efficiency inside your company's labor market pays enormous dividends if done correctly. Imagine the business outcomes you could drive if you knew every skill every person has inside your company right now. How quickly could you deploy resources to solve a problem? Who are the most qualified people to join the innovation task force? Where should your organization be developing skills against gaps? Who are the best people for the VP role? How well are new managers managing? How much could you reduce recruiting costs if you knew you were hiring against skills and not logos on a resume? How much could you improve employee retention? And, how important is it for your business to begin taking the measurement of skills seriously?

Three simple questions can guide your progress toward being able to speak the language of skills:

1. What skills do we have?
2. What skills do we need?
3. What could we do if we had this information at our fingertips?

If you can't answer these questions, then you are operating with an inefficient internal labor market and relying on more opaque signals of skills.

Skills as a Currency

The labor market transacts in much the same way as any other market does, using currency to translate relative value to make the market more

efficient. If skills are the unit of value in the labor market, then professional credentials are the currency. And there's the rub. There are so
many types of academic and professional credentials in the market today
that the market cannot transact with them effectively.

The market is flooded with different credentials: professional des-
ignations from associations (e.g., CPA, PMI, CAN), micro-degrees,
nano-degrees, company-specific certifications, open badges, and of
course the traditional college degree.

The problem with these credentials is that they all represent different things to different people. Some measure the completion of courses,
while others measure knowledge; some measure time spent doing something, while others are simply meaningless. But if you're hiring or promoting, how do you value a Microsoft MSCE certification against an
HP Master ASE Storage Solutions Architect Level 2 open badge? Or a
nano-degree from an online course provider? What skills do these represent? Do they represent skills or knowledge at all?

Right now, not enough companies are thinking about talent in terms
of skills, depending instead on formal degrees. More companies need to
find better ways for people to talk about the skills they have gained.

It's alphabet soup out there. What we need is a single currency to
measure any skill at any level, and provide workers, managers, and
recruiters with a common language in which to interact.

Degrees Plus Credentials

It doesn't have to be an either–or proposition when it comes to degrees and
credentials. Both can be valuable, but only if you can appreciate the skills
behind them and understand the financial tradeoffs. Salman Khan believes
that learning credentials go far beyond the traditional degree, especially
given the cost of Ivy League schools. Khan said, "A student pays $200,000 to
get a degree now, how do you justify that? The university might validate the
cost through the quality of their teaching or their impressive campus, but
they don't talk about the learning experience; and the students may argue
that spending $200,000 and four years of their lives is worth the credentials

at the end of it. There's definitely something broken when a large amount of money is changing hands and the buyer and the seller are selling and buying two different things."

If you could have a Harvard education *or* a Harvard degree, but not both, which would you choose?

Khan believes that another problem with traditional formal education is that it doesn't actually showcase to employers what you actually know. The traditional resumé goes some way toward conveying your learning experience. But some of it could be made up or grossly exaggerated. That's why Khan Academy is focusing on encouraging its participants to create portfolios that show the extent of their capabilities. These portfolios would include videos of people giving speeches, leading a project, or show reports from their peers or faculty advisers talking about what they were like to work with. This holistic approach is key to tapping into what colleges and employers are looking for today. As Khan said, "Colleges and employers today care about the portfolio of work, care about what other people think of the candidate, and have certain baseline expectations around content mastery. They also care about 'worldliness' and if you can show that worldliness in action."[13]

Skills Build Collective Intelligence and Ability

If skills are the building blocks of potential within your organization, then think about:

- The value you could derive if you knew what all of those skills were
- How you could apply all that collective knowledge
- The potential your company really has
- How efficient your company would be

For example, Janice has worked for a software company in product development for nearly a decade and has developed strong product design skills in her role. From time to time she is brought into key sales

meetings with prospects to articulate nuances of the product and to outline the product road map. When an internal job opens inside the sales
organization and ends up being filled by an external candidate, Janice
goes to HR to express her frustration at not being given visibility into
that opportunity or indeed the chance to interview for the position.

She expresses her desire to move into other fields besides product
design and how she would have really valued the opportunity to move
into sales, particularly when she already has a good reputation within the
sales team.

If this situation happens a few more times to Janice, the outcome is
predictable. Eventually, she will leave the company to find an opportunity that better matches her desired career path.

Instead of losing valuable employees like Janice, consider the following alternative: imagine posting a job and then running a report to see
the pool of next-most-qualified candidates based solely on how well their
skills match to the job opening. After seeing the report, you proactively
talk to managers and let them know a person on their team might be a
good fit—before running a recruiting process internally.

Then, you interview candidates to gauge their missions, visions, and
personal values. Thanks to your verified skills report, you can also use
the opportunity to assess the levels of team chemistry. After meeting
with candidates from finance, marketing, operations, sales, and product,
you hire someone from the marketing department who brings experience and perspective that creates empathy and brings a new dynamic
to the sales team. Since the candidate has all the company history and
context, she hits the ground running. Others inside the company who
didn't get the position learn that the company is now looking to hire high
performers with specific skills from within—something that motivates
them to continue to perform at high levels and develop more skills.

Each person in your company comes with a unique portfolio of skills
and level of mastery. And collectively, your company also possesses a
unique skill genome. Until you measure these skills, they are nothing but
intangible assets that cannot be managed, deployed, grown, or leveraged
to improve, adapt, innovate, or compete in the global market.

Measuring Skills

All organizations need to set standards to create a complete picture of how they are measuring and growing skills in particular roles. For example, when considering the role of a client implementation specialist, they could ask the following questions: What does it mean to be a successful client implementation specialist? What skills are required for the role and at what level of mastery? There are myriad taxonomies and tools available to help organizations find the answers to these questions by mapping job roles to skills. In fact, more and more companies are turning to AI and machine-learning technologies with relational databases to make recommendations based on near real-time labor market and jobs data.

According to the Lumina Foundation, "A lot has been written about the impact of technology and whether robots and artificial intelligence will supplant humans. Far less has been said about the opportunities that advances in technology will create for building new credentialing systems that can capture and validate all forms of learning."[14] The idea that we can validate all forms of learning is becoming widespread, and that is the goal.

Many companies are also setting mastery levels for the skills they've identified for each role. The Lumina Foundation's Connecting Credentials rubric is a popular eight-level rubric that is applicable to any skill and serves as a useful way to set standards and measure mastery. Once those standards are set, you can train against and measure the results of your efforts.

Telus International, a global telecom company, is using the Lumina rubric built into Degreed to measure the specific skills obtained by 300 employees taking part in a formal training program. Following the program, which includes a combination of several modalities of learning, project-based learning, and feedback sessions, everyone goes through a process to specifically measure and certify their skills.

The benefits of this process are twofold: individuals receive certifications for the skills they have gained, while the company gets a better idea of the effectiveness of the training program and the skills obtained for that team. These results are then benchmarked against the job roles for each person to see how well they map onto the expectations and needs of the business. As this program continues, the organization will be able to benchmark the development of skills over time, resulting in a rich data set that provides a mapped genome of skills inside the company that few others could match.

A growing number of companies like Telus recognize the massive value of the roles skill development and thoughtful measurement play when it comes to defining job success.

Skills Quotient (SQ)

Once these skills have been measured, then you can start to leverage the information to create a new dynamic in the company. We propose using a new standard we call the Skills Quotient, or SQ. The SQ is the skills you have divided by the skills you need (then multiplied by 100). Here's how you calculate an SQ:

1. Choose a role that you care about.
2. Identify the skills that matter for that role.
3. Identify the levels of these skills expected for that role.
4. Add up the levels in these skills expected for that role.
5. Measure your own level in these skills.
6. Add up your levels in these skills.
7. Divide the skills you have by the skills you need and multiply by 100.

For example, let's say you're a technical writer inside a software company. The company has outlined nine critical skills for you to master, each with a target mastery level (we'll use the Lumina Foundation's eight-level rubric for leveling), as Table 8.1 illustrates below:

Table 8.1   Lumina Foundation's eight-level rubric for leveling

Skill	Target Mastery Skill Level	Actual Verified Skill Level
Business Communications	5	4
Research	3	3
Time Management	4	3
Software Testing	3	4
Writing	7	6
Project Management	3	2
Editing	5	4
Computer Skills	6	4
Communication Skills	5	6 (caps at Target Level = 5)
TOTALS	**41**	**35**

In this example, your SQ for the role of technical writer at the company is 85—calculated by dividing the skills you already have (35), by the skills you need (41) and then multiplying by 100. You'll notice the caveat with "Communication Skills" where in this example, your skills exceed the target mastery skill level; in these cases where you have exceeded the target, the calculation never exceeds the target level.

An SQ of 100 means you have a perfect match between the required skills for your job, and the skills you have mastered. Of course, a score of 0 means you have none of the skills required for a particular job. Yet, it's worth noting that the SQ is always contextual. For example, you may have an SQ of 0 for the job of microbiologist, since you likely hold none of the skills required, but it does not mean you don't have any skills at all. The level of skills you have very much depends on the context in which they are applied. You wouldn't want to rely on skills that you can't use—just ask the people with PhDs who drive taxis or tend bars or people who've started to lose their jobs to automation.

The goal of the SQ is twofold: first, to measure how well-equipped a person is to perform at potential, that is to say, to measure the complete abilities of a body of workers against the work to be done; and second, to signal the potential threats and opportunities within an organization. For the former, it signals how ready you are, in the short-term, to deploy your skills against any of the initiatives or projects in your company. A score of 100 means you're as ready as can be; a score of 120 would mean you have lots of untapped skill in your organization; and a score of 50 means you're severely lacking in your ability to meet the demands you already have.

The second purpose of SQ is as a leading indicator of how engaged or frustrated your workers might be. For example, if you're in a role that requires eight skills at a specific level of mastery, and you have all those eight skills at the right mastery level (an SQ of 100), what are the chances that you're highly engaged in your work? Or conversely, what if you're in a job that requires those same skills but you're only proficient in two of them (an SQ of 35, for example)? You're likely going to be frustrated and probably end up failing, quitting, or being fired. People want to grow and to be challenged, but they need to have enough of a baseline to succeed as well as enough context to get to the right answers if they work hard. So, while a score of 100 might sound positive for the company in the short term, it also signifies lack of individual growth, which will have a negative effect on the company in the mid- to long-term.

Instead, organizations should aim for a balance between the company's need for adequate bench strength, and the ability to achieve business results and growth opportunities for individuals. An SQ range of 70–85 for most companies is ideal for creating both balance and tension. This score allows enough depth for people to be successful in their jobs while still providing opportunities for growth at individual, team, departmental, and companywide levels. In other words, this SQ range enables your organization to burn orange-hot—hot enough to make great progress and challenge people, but not so hot to burn people out, or so cold that they lose momentum.

It's also worth noting the business benefits to using SQ as an operating function. SQ answers questions such as *What skills do you have? What skills do you lack?* It gives you the data to make business decisions based on your skills. The SQ can be used to measure growth of the:

- Labor market
- Industry
- Company
- Department
- Individual

It's something that's never been possible before, but in today's knowledge economy, what could be more powerful?

How to Use the Skills Quotient (SQ)

This section contains several hypothetical case studies of how companies can use SQ in a practical way to help understand the skills they have versus the skills they need.

Job seeking

A skilled retail manager works for a company that has succumbed to pressure from a large online retailer. Since the entire industry is contracting, there just aren't enough management jobs to go around. The manager works with a placement agency to do a comprehensive skills assessment, which measures the skills he has developed over the past 27 years. The agency then calculates his skills quotient against a large database of open roles, then recommends that the manager apply to those roles with a skills quotient above 70 with the highest starting salary.

Recruiting

A solar company needs to hire 200 solar installers across several states, but it has thousands of applications. Since it is a forward-looking company, they don't want to exclude people who don't have college degrees, but they still need to filter this list down to those who are most qualified for the role. To find the most suitable candidate, they direct each applicant to a skills assessment portal that measures their skill levels against the skills necessary for the solar installer role. The solar company measures the skills quotient for each applicant and interviews those with the highest values. Since all applicants' measurements are recorded in a lifelong transcript, even those who do not get the job can walk away with evidence of their skills that will help them in their quest for another job.

Internal recruiting

At a 150-year-old traditional tech company, an experienced VP of sales has decided to retire without a clear succession plan in place. However, the sales organization recently did a full skills inventory as part of their annual development process, where each member rated themselves against a set of relevant skills. As a first pass, this company calculates the self-reported skills quotient for each member against the VP of sales role. Those who rank highest then go through a rigorous "Skill Certification" process for several of the most important skills, to verify that their self-assessments are truthful and unbiased. One of these high achievers is chosen to fill the vacant position, and the remainder leave with clear direction as to where they need to grow to be ready for the next big opportunity.

Contract assignment

A large consulting firm needs a better way to match employees with time available to open contracts. Since this is their core business, they've already assessed the skills their employees have by tying voluntary development of high-demand skills to significant incentive bonuses. To improve the contract assignment process, they treat each contract as a role, identifying with the stakeholders the type of skills and skill levels needed for that role. They then calculate a skills quotient for all available employees, looking for values close to 100 for maximum customer satisfaction.

Promotion list

A multinational manufacturer of products focuses heavily on promoting top performers, doing their best to ensure that each high-potential employee has opportunities for growth somewhere in the corporate family. Since all top performers go through a comprehensive skills assessment and regularly update their progress, the company calculates the SQ for each top performer against their current role. Anyone with an SQ above 90 gets flagged for immediate review. Why? Because these high performers will likely look for their next growth opportunity elsewhere if they aren't given one within the company.

Reskilling initiative

A large global consulting company sees emerging trends in data science and decides they need to provide service professionals who can fill those roles. However, there just aren't enough data scientists around to hire the thousands needed to fill customer demand. Since the company needs to know what skills their employees have to match them to contracts, they have a skills inventory integrated into onboarding, with ongoing skill measurement playing an integral part of their talent development plan. With this data available, the company measures a skills quotient for each employee against a data scientist role, quickly identifying whom they could develop to fill the gap.

Mentoring program

A Silicon Valley social media company has a loose matrix organization and has decided to promote mentoring across the company. For each employee, the company identifies the skill with the largest deficit between their current skill level and the skill level expected for their role. It then identifies three people in the same location with both a higher level in that skill and the largest surplus between the actual and expected skill levels for that skill. These mentors and mentees then meet in person to see who would be the best personality fit. The mentees make rapid progress getting up to speed, and the mentors derive satisfaction from using an underutilized skill to support someone else.

Skills inventory

A software tech giant wants to identify which skills training would be of most benefit to employees. As part of a companywide initiative, every employee in the company is asked to identify their five strongest skills and rate their current level in those skills. In addition, the managers in the company are responsible for defining the expected skills and skill levels needed for each role, so that these requirements can be included in each job posting. With this information available, the company adds up the skills people have and divides that by the skills people need for each skill across the organization. They then subtract these skills quotients from 100 and multiply by the number of people who need each skill.

Sorting the results from greatest to least quickly highlights the specific skills where employees could use additional learning. The company then searches a large content aggregator for those skills, filtering by the skill levels that most need improvement, and finds high-quality content that meets many of their needs. For the remaining needs, they use internal learning design experts and their own subject matter experts to create custom content, perfectly suited to their own business needs.

Training assessment

The executive team at an online marketplace chooses management quality as their top development initiative for 2020. To move the needle, they've decided that each manager will go through several intensive training programs with follow-up spread throughout the year. At the beginning of the year, a random sample of managers goes through a rigorous evaluation process, measuring their levels in five key management skills. At the end of the year, they repeat this process, applying everything they've learned. The company calculates their average skills quotient at the beginning of the year and at the end of the year, showing the real impact of the training program on the overall quality of management at the company.

Degree programs

A prestigious technical university has identified a critical set of skills and skill levels that they want all graduates of their supply chain management master's program to achieve. To accomplish this goal, all graduates go through a rigorous skill measurement process for each of these critical skills as part of their last semester before graduation. Those skills that have the lowest actual levels relative to their expected levels get extra attention, with relevant projects incorporated into several core courses. Over time, the university calculates the skills quotient of each graduate against the target skill set to track as program quality improves.

Summary

Making expertise count in the knowledge economy is gaining more traction from all sectors—universities, companies, and individuals. We all want a better way to be able to talk about what we know and what we can do. A common language of skills will help us all communicate effectively so recruiters can screen candidates better and managers can hire the right talent, so leaders can get the right people into the right jobs at the right times, and so individuals have a way to navigate their careers over their lifetimes.

The Future Is Already Here

IMAGINE LIVING IN a world where people don't have to work anymore, where people work because they want to. All work is a hobby, and all the necessities of life and happiness are available because the world is so productive. While this may sound like the stuff of science fiction, Alan Walton believes that the growing sophistication of machines will eventually turn this vision into a reality.

Walton is a senior data scientist who invented and helped build a human-machine hybrid system that measures any skill in any field at any level of expertise. He is always learning and building his own skills, and in the past few years he has been focusing on data science and machine learning, which then led him to dive head on into the field of deep learning. Deep learning focuses on sophisticated networks: deep neural networks, deep belief networks, and recurrent neural networks. These networks are applied to fields such as speech recognition, natural language processing, image recognition, audio recognition, and computer vision to name a few. He is now focusing on deep learning to imagine the workforce 100 years into the future.

Walton emphasizes, "We need computers to be able to do more things that only humans can do right now. And then when you think about the tools that let computers do more things, deep learning is *the* tool right now. It's drastically expanding what computers can do."[1]

When deep learning is applied in the real world, it can generate some powerful results. Deep learning powers Facebook's image recognition technology when you post pictures, Google's translate technology[2] that instantly translates more than 100 languages almost as well as humans, and Deep Instinct's powerful cybersecurity learning algorithms[3] that predict and detect computer system threats.

Google's artificial intelligence (AI) research group, DeepMind, is perhaps the most influential in pushing the boundaries of artificial intelligence. In 2017, an award-winning documentary showcased Deep-Mind's AlphaGo system, which learned the sophisticated ancient Chinese game of "Go" so well that it beat South Korean grandmaster Lee Sedol, considered orders of magnitude better than any other Go player in the world. The game of Go is an abstract war simulation created in China 2,500 years ago. It is simple and yet complex; its complexity comes from the fact that the possibilities of play are almost endless. It has taken 2,500 years for humans to master the game, while DeepMind's team of more than 100 scientists[4] created a distributed system that used deep learning to beat the grandmaster in just three years.

What's interesting about the human-versus-machine story is how prominently human emotions come into play. Sedol admitted that he felt hindered by his "humanness." Before the game began, he was the world champion, confident in the knowledge that he would triumph over the machine. Even after he lost the first game, he still believed he could outmaneuver his nonhuman adversary. Yet, as the game went on, Sedol struggled to sense what the machine was doing; he overthought his strategy and, consequently, became tense and insecure. When Sedol lost four games to one, he was emotional. He tried to stay composed and apologized for letting everyone down. Ultimately, he accepted defeat by machine.

DeepMind's next version of the technology is called AlphaGo Zero, a supercomputer that has learned by playing itself millions of times without any human intervention beyond giving it the rules of the game. David Silver, AlphaGo's lead researcher, said, "It's more powerful than previous approaches because by not using human data, or human expertise in any fashion, we've removed the constraints of human knowledge and it is able to create knowledge itself."[5] With AlphaGo Zero, computers are now teaching humans how to play the game of Go.

Advances in deep learning are moving quickly. It has been only two decades since IBM's computer DeepBlue beat world chess champion Garry Kasparov in a chess match, and less than eight years since IBM's Watson beat the world champions at the game of Jeopardy. The rapid progression—machines learning from humans to Google's DeepMind supercomputer learning entirely on its own—illustrates the unbelievable evolution of technology, an evolution that will move even faster once we learn to debunk the "intelligence myth."

The Intelligence Myth

Economist Daniel Susskind, author of *The Future of the Professions: How Technology Will Transform the Work of Human Experts*,[6] believes that we need to challenge the "intelligence myth," which is the "the belief that machines have to copy the way human beings think and reason."[7] Not long ago, it was thought that certain nonroutine tasks just couldn't be automated and that humans would continue to perform those tasks. But recent technology has demonstrated otherwise. Cars don't need human drivers, machines can accurately diagnose some types of cancer and suggest treatment options, and as the Go example shows, computers can beat humans in complex "thinking" challenges.

Susskind said that resolving the intelligence myth will show us that our "limited understanding about human intelligence, about how we think and reason, is far less a constraint than it was in the past."[8] What's more, since we don't completely understand human intelligence, there's no reason to think that we know what machines might be capable of doing in the future.

Yet thinking about what machines could be capable of is a daunting prospect for many. After all, it can be scary to think that machines will take over the professions and careers of the future—that our teachers, doctors, and drivers could be replaced with machines. But we shouldn't see machines as being a threat. When human intelligence is augmented with machines and technology, we get the best of both worlds. It doesn't have to be an either/or proposition.

World-renowned chess champion Garry Kasparov, who lost to a machine in 1997, makes this case. Since his well-known chess match, he's done a lot of thinking himself about humanity and machines. Kasparov said that "as always, machine's triumph was a human triumph—something we tend to forget when humans are surpassed by our own creations."[9]

In other words, given that humans created the machines in the first place, we should celebrate their achievements. What's most important, according to Kasparov, "is how we humans feel about living and working with these machines."[10]

Machines have objectivity, can make calculations, and take instruction, but humans have understanding, purpose, and passion. Computers can't show compassion or empathy or deep human emotions crucial for basic survival, building relationships, and creating community—yet. When human and machine intelligence are combined, they have the power to create incredible things.

Like Walton, Kasparov believes that "we will need the help of new intelligent machines to turn our grandest dreams into reality." Machines and technology will give us new options in the work that we do and how we live our lives. And learning will continue to play a huge role in this future.

Careers that Haven't Yet Been Invented

When we think about work, jobs, and careers, it's hard to predict where the world will go next. A little more than a decade ago, Apple iPhones were just being introduced; they've changed our lives in ways we couldn't have imagined. Today, most of us can't live without mobile phones and computers in our pockets. In tandem, the job market has changed significantly. Jobs like driverless car engineers and YouTube content creators didn't exist 10 years ago, and if you have kids who are younger than five, 65 percent of them are likely to end up in jobs and careers that haven't yet been invented.[11]

So, when we think about the skills of the future, it's difficult to predict exactly what people will need. Because of that, we have to think less about the traditional view of careers as job roles and job descriptions and more about the skills people will need to solve the world's most pressing problems. This is why learning and continuously building skills are so important. It's why employees need to be agile learners to keep up with, and be prepared for, what's new and how technology is advancing in the world. Skills are currency in the expertise economy, and the most successful companies are already thinking about this and putting strategies in place—these will be the companies that will thrive in an uncertain future.

Skills for the Future

There are certain skills and knowledge that will be valuable for the future even with the rise of artificial intelligence and machine learning. Andrew Scott, professor at the London School of Economics and co-author of *The 100-Year Life: Living and Working in an Age of Longevity*, identifies three key areas where education and learning can support the careers of the future:

1. Supporting the development of ideas and creativity
2. Enabling human skills and empathy
3. Developing mental flexibility and agility[12]

Scott also predicts that technology will greatly impact the education sector. Classroom teaching and textbooks will be replaced with digital, adaptable versions (this has already happened in many schools), and the emphasis will instead focus on how educators and trainers can motivate, empathize, and encourage learning.[13] The way we learn will also change. It will be much less about what we know (since knowledge acquisition becomes easier through technology), but rather what we do with what we know that will prove most important. Mastery and evidence of skills, not degrees, will be the future currency.

Sal Khan, founder of the Khan Academy, agrees. He believes that building a portfolio that showcases what we can actually do is going to be a key differentiator: "It will be exciting to see someone's portfolio creation. 'Hey, here's a prompt: Why don't you build this, write this, do this, video this, and when you do it, you get some feedback and opportunities to revise.' You can imagine that if you have all this in the next 10 years, you're only going to be limited by your time and your motivation."

One of the goals of the Khan Academy is to reach motivated people around the globe and make it possible for them to receive an education they otherwise could not pursue. Khan elaborates: "We have people on Khan Academy who are refugees, but they are so motivated that they literally go from K–12 in three years and become an engineer." In other words, a highly motivated person is now able to pursue an education and unlock career opportunities previously impossible to imagine with the constraints of finances and geography.

Khan also believes that the Khan Academy platform can help motivate people, since "anyone who literally wants to learn anything will be able to start at any level, get explanations, get practice, get game mechanics—they will be able to learn whatever they want to learn. And they will be able to prove what they know to the world, and that proof will be directly connected to opportunities. So that's exciting!"[14]

Skills and the Gig Economy

Scott, in *The 100-Year Life*, states that in the future, technology that connects an individual to companies who want to buy their skills will become more global, cheaper, and more sophisticated. These connecting platforms are already proliferating, leading to growing commentary about the "gig economy" and the "sharing economy." It's possible right now to sell almost any skill across the market.[15]

To illustrate Scott's point, when Kelly travels on business trips, she uses Airbnb for her accommodation, Uber for all her transportation in Europe, Lyft for getting around in the United States, and Rover.com as a pet-sitting service for her dogs. Conveniently, the same person from Rover.com also works as a driver for Lyft and, as an independent worker, is able to control what work she does, flex her work schedule, and decide how much money she makes. This is the gig economy in action.

The number of workers in the gig economy continues to grow. Some are doing it part time, some full time. As people start to think about marketing and selling their skills for projects or short-term jobs in the future, it becomes even more important that we have a common understanding of what skills people have and a common way to think and talk about them.

What about the Baby Boomers?

While a huge focus has been on predicting the future of technology, comparatively little has been devoted to the future of humans—particularly in the case of the baby boomer generation. Karie Willyerd, a workplace futurist, predicted future trends in the world of learning and work in her book *The 2020 Workplace: How Innovative Companies Attract, Develop, and Keep Tomorrow's Employees Today*. It's interesting to look back and see how the predictions have panned out. She notes that eight years ago the world was worried about baby boomers retiring *en masse*, but with the combination of the great recession forcing people to work longer and the fact that, in general, careers last longer because we are living longer, baby boomers are *not* leaving the workforce. They are not as prepared financially as they need to be, so there are a lot more baby boomers in the workforce, and we have not necessarily prepared for that or accommodated for that. [16]

People not only need to work longer, they actually *want* to work longer. Many people who have retired say the one thing they regret is that they retired too early and that retirement is overrated. Willyerd said, "People want to have a meaningful contribution to society, and if it's not through their work, it's going to be through giving back in some other way. They may change how they work, but they plan on working longer."[17]

People also go through different life stages. In one stage an employee can be "all in" on a career. At any one time a person has different things that they need to attend to in life. For example, Willyerd explains, "Say you have aging parents, or you just had a set of twins one year after your other baby was born, and so maybe you have to go a little bit slower. But does that mean you have to get off the career ladder if you can't keep climbing as fast as others? You should be able to learn and go at your own pace."[18]

Finding purpose in life through work is not just for the younger workforce, either. For her book *Stretch: How to Future-Proof Yourself for Tomorrow's Workplace*,[19] Willyerd interviewed six people who were more than 100 years old. When she talked to them, it was all about what they were going to do next. "It's the nature of the healthy human being who is thinking, 'Ok, what else do I need to do?'"

For other people, the dream was to keep the job they had. Willyerd said, "Nobody owns a job. There is no such thing as 'my job' unless you are the entrepreneur who started the company, because jobs belong to companies."[20] So, the message is that if you want the job you have, you have to keep up with how the job is shifting and changing.

Nigel Paine, author of *The Learning Challenge*, agrees that we haven't put nearly enough emphasis on the working population over 50. "What we've got now is a super obsession with everyone who is under 30—and we've got to think about them, worry about them, build for them, and make sure they're on board. What we are *not* doing is making sure that the 50- and 60-year-olds are on board with the sometimes 20 more years of their career. We still have that idea that when you reach 50 you are pretty much redundant and it's hopeless."

The mindset change that needs to happen in companies is substantial. Our society, in general, doesn't value older workers, and Paine reminds us that "we've extended the working career, but we haven't extended the working career mentality. In other words, we expect people might work until they are 70, but we write them off at the age of 50." The ageism is real and it's going to become a bigger problem over the next decades. We need to value this demographic as contributing members of the workforce. They want and need to be working, and they provide a level of expertise that comes from experience that you just don't get with someone a few years out of school.

The employees in this age group also can be amazing mentors and share what they know and can do with others. Instead, Paine says, "Organizations are wasting a vast amount of human potential because they are telling [older] people to take it easy, don't worry, and just do their job." What they should be saying is, "Hey, here's a new challenge, let's develop you, let's look at a career shift, let's look at a new job, let's keep you motivated and excited for the next 10 to 15 years."[21]

Lynda Gratton, co-author of *The 100-Year Life*, makes the case that "we need to abandon the traditional idea of a neatly arranged, three-staged life comprised of education, career, and retirement. Instead, we need to embrace a multiple-phased life course where people keep learning throughout their lives, take lots of breaks, and dip in and out of jobs and careers."[22]

Joining Forces to Tackle the Skills Gap

No single company, university, person, group, or even one generation can solve the skills gap issue alone. We also can't address the skills issue in isolation since each area is so dependent on the others for success. So, we need to tackle skills, learning, and education where they all meet: at the intersection of universities, companies, and individuals. Each has a part to play. It's not a solution that overhauls any one of these systems, but rather the solution lies in connecting these systems in a more deliberate way.

In general, these forces all have similar high-level goals—to help solve the skills gap and help society become more educated, productive, and successful. But it's tough. Learning and education is multifaceted, sometimes polarizing, and complex. Yet, there are countless ideas percolating in relative isolation today that could inform what others are thinking and doing around learning transformation.

It's possible, however, to make some progress and think about how these three forces can be more in sync with where we are all headed. We think there is a way for universities to do their part, for companies to remain competitive, and for individuals to get the best chance to realize their career goals and dreams by joining forces and taking new and fresh approaches to learning. The following sections are high-level recommendations on what we can do as universities, companies, and individuals to prepare for skills as the currency of the expertise economy.

What Universities Can Do

Universities are incredibly expensive, and "Is it worth it?" is the question students and parents ask most often. Are universities preparing students with skills they need to be successful in the workforce? Universities weren't originally formed to help people get jobs. Instead, they were created to help educate so we could all be more informed citizens of the world. However, as we moved from the days of Socrates and Plato to the Industrial Revolution and now into the knowledge and expertise economy, universities have, sometimes reluctantly, taken on another role.

Studies show that in this economy, college-educated people have an advantage in the workforce. According to the Economic Policy Institute, college graduates, on average, earned 56 percent more than high school grads in 2015.[23] Thirty-three percent of Americans are college graduates and are paying hundreds of thousands of dollars to land a more successful job and generate more income over their lifetimes. As tuition costs have risen and student debts have climbed in tandem, students are increasingly asking universities for more than just theoretical information; they want practical information to help them get a job and succeed once they land it.

We haven't yet filled the gap between what students learn in college and what they need to do practically to be successful in the workplace. But there are ways to connect higher education more closely with the real needs of companies without completely overhauling it or discarding it, thus giving students a better shot at gaining the relevant skills for the job market.

1. Universities should stay connected with graduates

Universities are typically subject-based and not career-based. Students can major in math or computer science, marketing or public relations, and it gives them a solid foundation for a career. But they still need professional development along the way. Colleges tend to say goodbye to students as they graduate and, typically, only get back in touch for alumni group participation or for donations. But students' education doesn't end when they graduate. In fact, it's just beginning, especially given that most people could be in the workforce for 50 to 60 years.

So, what happens to graduates who want to learn more during their careers? Jaime Casap, education evangelist at Google, says "…people don't go back to their university when they need professional development. Instead, they turn to their company or to other solutions like Degreed or Khan Academy. So, if you spent four or more years in higher education, a place that influenced the direction of your life, those schools should be a place you feel connected to and want to get more from."

Casap tells the story of his daughter, Elaine. She graduated from college two years ago, and she hasn't been contacted by her university since. Casap wonders why she isn't getting an email a year later asking, "'Hey Elaine, what are you doing today? Oh, you're working in video production at the *New York Times*. We just scanned through your transcript and there are some updates to the skills you learned since you graduated, and here's a refresher course on production skills. Or, 'We noticed that you didn't take journalism and you are now in that field, so here's a journalism class you might want to take. Oh, and by the way, there are nine other people in your university that live in New York, and they are also interested in taking a journalism class, why don't you all take a program together?'"[24] While this might seem like a big shift, helping universities stay connected to graduates throughout their careers benefits both parties.

2. Universities should partner with companies

While there are some exceptions, many colleges and universities haven't done enough to help new graduates prepare for the workforce and haven't

aligned degree programs to help students get entry-level jobs after graduation. Even though there are over six million open jobs available, new
college graduates are struggling to put their education to work. Forty
percent are underemployed and not getting jobs that use what they just
learned.[25] There's a great opportunity to partner more closely with companies to understand what's happening in the workforce and understand
what skills students will need to be successful and help close the gap of
what employers expect.

Even when graduates do get jobs, they are often ill equipped to meet
company expectations. According to a survey by Payscale, "More than
half of all companies (60 percent) said new grads lacked critical-thinking
skills and attention to detail (56 percent), while 44 percent found fault
with their writing proficiency, and 39 percent were critical of their public
speaking ability."[26] There is a great opportunity for universities to partner more closely with companies to help bridge the gap between what
companies want from their employees, and what those employees need
to be successful.

The public relations program at the University of Oregon is a great
example of how universities can partner with companies to help new
graduates prepare for the workforce. Seniors spend their final year working with real companies as clients. Students build a portfolio of their
work and present it to a panel of not only PR professors at the university,
but also PR professionals in the industry. By the time they have finished
the year, the seniors have had exposure working on a real project for an
actual company, practiced presenting in a high-pressure situation, and
received valuable feedback on their work. This provides them with some
of the experience they need to prepare them for the real world of work.

3. Universities should use emerging technology

Some universities are doing an incredible job of using technology to
help their students learn. Online undergraduate and graduate programs
provide students with the opportunities to learn anywhere, and at their
own pace. This is especially beneficial for those who want to earn their
master's degree because learning online or with a combination of online

and in-person meetings means they don't have to take a two-year career break to pursue an MBA.

The best learning programs in higher education use technology like video and collaboration tools to help participants learn from both professors and peers. In these cases, students are immersed in learning about new subjects, practice skills, get feedback, and reflect on what they learned (the Learning Loop model). The least-effective programs make people sit through unengaging online content or just put professor lectures online. Despite some lapses in quality, online education is becoming more and more popular, and it may end up displacing some of our more traditional institutions.

Clayton Christensen, Harvard Business School professor and author of *The Innovator's Dilemma*,[27] believes that online education will eventually disrupt higher education. The environment for disruption is created when a firm or industry begins to over-serve its customer base, creating space for entrants to offer "good-enough" solutions that are generally more affordable, accessible, and convenient for other tiers of customers. Universities generally overshoot on the needs of both employers and students, and as a result corporate education presents a disruptive opportunity.

Christensen also sees credentials for lifelong learning playing a huge role in the future of education. He believes that there are some jobs where a Harvard education just isn't necessary. So that's where credentials come in. "We see this phenomenon in higher education, and skill certification is a great example of how modular, plug-and-play pieces for skills and credentials has the potential to disrupt the degree."[28]

What Companies Can Do

Most companies know they are not getting college grads who are ready to hit the ground running when they enter the workforce, and their corporate training dollars are often wasted on misaligned training focused on the wrong things. However, there are three ways that companies can skill the workforce:

- Companies are at the cutting edge of new technology, which means that they can move faster than universities in helping people acquire new skills.
- Hiring managers can use skills as the new currency for evaluating candidates for job opportunities rather than just basing them on their pedigree.
- Managers can work with their employees to make sure they stay hungry and engaged by encouraging them to grow, learn, and transform their careers.

1. Companies can move fast to skill the workforce

Companies have traditionally been consumers of education and learning. They depend on universities to train the people they hire. Then, in the workforce, they expect their employees to learn on the job, with some management training thrown in. But, as the age of acceleration is moving ever faster, universities can't keep up with teaching the latest technologies and methodologies. For example, when mobile software development became a highly desired skill, companies couldn't rely on universities to teach students about the latest mobile technology, so it was left to them to build talent from within.

But, what if companies could become producers as well as consumers of education? Some companies are already doing this. For example, for decades General Electric, not Harvard, was known for producing the best leaders in their industry. Some of the best business training comes from the consulting firm McKinsey, not Wharton. If we now think about technologies like cybersecurity, cryptocurrency, deep learning, and artificial intelligence, companies that are deeply immersed in these technologies could help people build skills for a specialty area and develop talent for a whole industry, not just for the company itself.

2. Don't hire for pedigree—hire for real skills

Hiring managers have a huge role to play in the future of learning and skills. They are the lynchpin. If managers continue to hire based on signals besides skills such as what school their employees went to (Stanford or Harvard, for instance), their GPA, or the brand of the company they worked for previously (one of the big tech giants), the skills gap will persist.

Leaders need to elevate skills and what people can actually *do* over pedigree. The fact that someone got a degree in communications or economics from Columbia 10 years ago doesn't tell you anything valuable about their skills today or what they can actually do. Hiring managers should focus on people's ability and desire to continuously learn new things—learning agility should be top of the list of desired skills.

3. Once you hire them, help your employees stay hungry

Whether working with a new college grad or a seasoned professional, managers need to continuously challenge their employees so that companies can stay competitive. This means understanding that there is a cycle every employee goes through when they start a new job or assignment.

According to Whitney Johnson, author of *Build an A-Team: Play to Their Strengths and Lead Them Up the Learning Curve*,[29] "Everyone is on a learning curve, or an S curve, in their current role. Initially you are inexperienced, then you move into engagement, and then finally mastery." Companies can help employees stay engaged and hungry by understanding where their employees are on this curve.

At the low end of the curve, typically between six months and a year on the job, people are the most inexperienced and still unsure about what they are doing. Johnson says, "You want to have about 15 percent of your workforce or your team at any given time at this low end of the curve of inexperience, because they are going to be questioning everything that they are seeing. And when they are questioning everything they are seeing, it often leads to a better way of doing things. So that's the curve of inexperience."[30]

Following this stage is the engagement phase of the curve, which lasts two to three years. This is where most people become more competent and confident. "You want to have about 70 percent of your team on this part of the curve at any given time," says Johnson. "They know enough that they are capable, but not too much, so their neurons are still firing, but they are not yet bored. You manage these people by really looking for the stretch assignments."

During the mastery phase of the curve, "Your employee knows what they are doing, things are easy. The brain is no longer enjoying the feel-good effects of learning; they get bored."[31]

To keep employees hungry to learn and grow more, the mastery phase needs to become a launching pad to their next curve. As leaders and managers, we want them to become novices again where they begin to question everything and wonder how to do things differently. Then they move into engagement again and the cycle starts over.

The ideal workforce is made up of 70 percent of people in the sweet spot of engagement, 15 percent in the low end of inexperience, and 15 percent at mastery phase. As a company, if you are about to be disrupted, you should take the pulse of your workforce. Too many people at the high end of that curve leads to boredom and complacency. Bored and complacent people don't innovate; they get disrupted.

What Individuals Can Do

Often, individuals are not set up for success either from the universities or the companies that employ them. People need to take education and learning into their own hands and ultimately be responsible for their own career and job success. As Willyerd says, "There's no magic person behind the curtain thinking about your career—*it's all up to you!*"[32]

The consumerization of content, combined with the standardization of a common language for skills, leads to several benefits. People can continuously build expertise; receive quality, relevant education for less money; and earn credit for what they learn, all the while gaining skills for their current roles as well as their future careers. There are four ways individuals can take control of their own learning:

1. Invest in their own learning to build expertise
2. Treat learning as a form of exercise

3. Seek out mentors and role models
4. Create a learning profile

1. Continuously build expertise

For individuals, the best strategy is to continuously build skills and expertise. Individuals need to take control of their own career future and learning. In a 2016 survey,[33] Manpower cites that 93 percent of Millennials are willing to spend their own money on further training that they are not getting from universities and employers. Leaders and managers need to reinforce the message of their employees taking ownership over their own learning and careers, but also help guide them along the way.

2. Treat learning like exercise

Some people love learning, just as some people love exercising and going to the gym. If you want to get results, if you want to better yourself, it takes work. Sometimes it will make you uncomfortable and sometimes it will be hard. It's painful to learn and grow, but once you get into a learning routine, improving your mind starts to feel good. Khan noted that 30 to 40 years ago it was not mainstream for people to go to the gym regularly. If you were in a sport at school, you might go, but when you're out of school, most people did not go to the gym in a semi-regular way. Then, in the 1980s, mindset shifted, and going to the gym became part of people's routine. Khan says, "I think that's a direct analogy to learning."

Technology like Degreed and Khan Academy can be like your gym for learning—a way to exercise your brain. Khan says, "The most important thing is to set aside time, just like you would do for the gym, and say, 'I'm going to do 30 minutes of learning every day.' And it's frankly much easier to learn these days because you can get it on your mobile phone, or any device, and you can do both at the same time—oxygen flowing to the brain is great for learning."[34]

3. Find mentors and role models

If you ask successful people what has had the biggest impact on their career, you'll often hear them talk about their mentors and role models. Many companies have tried to create mentoring programs without much success. Johnson, executive coach and author of *Disrupt Yourself: Putting the Power of Disruptive Innovation to Work*,[35] believes that finding the right mentor is a similar process to dating: there has to be some level of chemistry. "It's a dating-style relationship at some level. As the mentor, I think there's actually got to be something in the person you want to invest time in. Frequently, it's that the person is a shinier, sleeker version of you, so it is fun to mentor them. There is also this sense of hunger, and you want to help the next generation. In mentoring, it is giving something to you in terms of the legacy you want to create."

Technology is making it easier to unlock some of the limitations of traditional mentoring. For example, on MasterClass.com, they offer courses by basketball player Steph Curry and actress Helen Mirren. Johnson says, "I signed up for the Helen Mirren one on acting, not because I want to be an actor but because I thought it would help me improve my public speaking. Is she mentoring me? Well, yeah, kind of. I consider that mentoring. Listening to audiobooks, webinars—these are ways we can be mentored. Yes, there is the personal element, but I think for me oftentimes it becomes more of a one-off."[36]

4. Create a Learning Profile

In the expertise economy, skills are king. We are knowledge workers in a knowledge economy, yet we can't tell you what we learned last year. So how do you talk about your skills and how do you show what you've been learning every year, every month, every day? How do you take your learning and skills with you as you move along your career journey?

Learning isn't just about a college degree—whether you have one or not. It's about what you know and what you can do with what you know. Degreed allows you to create your learning profile so that you can discover, track, and measure all your learning—formal and informal.

Although you can add your formal degrees to your profile, you can also add everything you learn day to day, like the latest article you read or your favorite podcast or book—all the informal learning that is available. Degreed's learning profile can also track your career-long learning credentials. It helps you see the skills you have, the skills you need, and the skills you are building. You can use your learning profile as a personalized view to track your career goals, or use it to talk to your manager, your peers, or potential employers about what skills you have and what you can do.

A learning profile is not about replacing the college degree. On the contrary, a learning profile helps communicate what you've learned and what you are learning over the lifetime of your career. The future doesn't care how you became an expert, only that you did. You will continuously build skills over the course of your life, and you want a good way to be able to talk about that.

Learners Inherit the Earth

The expertise economy is a future where we all learn together over the entirety of our lives, where learning enables us to remain competitive in a world changing at advancing rates. In the words of the American philosopher Eric Hoffer, "In times of change learners inherit the earth; while the learned find themselves beautifully equipped for a world that no longer exists."

We have all been impacted by learning and education in some way. Great teachers, leaders, and mentors help shape our worldview and support us along our learning journey. Companies have the opportunity to play a huge part in this transformation in our lives and can play a huge part in making learning and education the best it can be—available for everyone who wants and needs it to succeed. Education not only leads to economic success, but also helps to solve the world's most pressing problems. In the expertise economy, we all have a responsibility to help teach and guide each other for our collective success.

ENDNOTES

Introduction

1. "Oracle Buys Sun," Oracle, April 20, 2009, http://www.oracle.com/us/corporate/press/018363.
2. Molly Brown, "Zuckerberg's Not-So-Subtle Message to Facebook Employees: Don't End up Like Sun Microsystems," Geekwire, December 8, 2014, https://www.geekwire.com/2014/zuckerbergs-not-subtle-message-facebook-employees-dont-end-like-sun-microsystems/.
3. Scott D. Anthony, S. Patrick Viguerie, Evan I. Schwartz and John Van Landeghem, "2018 Corporate Longevity Forecast: Creative Destruction is Accelerating," Innosight, https://www.innosight.com/insight/creative-destruction/.
4. Pablo Illanes, Susan Lund, Mona Mourshed, Scott Rutherford, and Magnus Tyreman, "Retraining and Reskilling Workers in the Age of Automation," McKinsey Global Institute, January 2018, https://www.mckinsey.com/global-themes/future-of-organizations-and-work/retraining-and-reskilling-workers-in-the-age-of-automation.
5. Ibid.
6. Ibid.
7. Jonathan Munk, "Universities Can't Solve Our Skills Gap Problem Because They Caused It," TechCrunch, May 8, 2016, https://techcrunch.com/2016/05/08/universities-cant-solve-our-skills-gap-problem-because-they-caused-it/.
8. Quentin Hardy, "Gearing Up for the Cloud, AT&T Tells Its Workers: Adapt, or Else," *New York Times,* February 13, 2016, Tech, https://www.nytimes.com/2016/02/14/technology/gearing-up-for-the-cloud-att-tells-its-workers-adapt-or-else.html?ref=technology&_r=1&mtrref=www.nytimes.com.
9. Tim Munden (chief learning officer, Unilever), interview by Kelly Palmer, March 2018.

Chapter 1

1. Bror Saxberg (vice president of learning science, Chan-Zuckerberg Initiative (CZI)), interview by Kelly Palmer, November 2017.

2. Ibid.

3. Ibid.

4. Ibid.

5. Artin Atabaki, Stacey Dietsch, and Julia M. Sperling, "How to Separate Learning Myths from Reality," McKinsey.com, July 2015, Organization, https://www.mckinsey.com/business-functions/organization/our-insights/how-to-separate-learning-myths-from-reality.

6. Julia Sperling, "McKinsey on Neuroscience and Learning," YouTube, https://www.youtube.com/watch?v=vp60MMtJ_30&ab_channel=McKinsey LD (Accessed March 14, 2018).

7. "The Learning Brain. Your Brain Is You: Learning & Education," BioEd Online, May 9, 2013, https://www.youtube.com/watch?v=27ZsQ9PjSW0 (Accessed March 14, 2018).

8. Julia Sperling, "McKinsey on Neuroscience and Learning," YouTube, https://www.youtube.com/watch?v=vp60MMtJ_30&ab_channel=McKinsey LD (Accessed March 14, 2018) (Accessed March 14, 2018).

9. Ibid.

10. Melanie Curtin, "Want to Strengthen Your Brain? Neuroscience Says to Start Reading this Immediately," Inc.com, https://www.inc.com/melanie-curtin/want-to-improve-brain-functioning-neuroscience-says-to-start-reading-this-immedi.html (Accessed March 14, 2018).

11. Todd Rose, *The End of Average: How We Succeed in a World that Values Sameness* (New York: HarperOne, 2016).

12. Ibid.

13. Maria Konnikova, "Does Thinking Fast Mean You're Thinking Smarter?" *Smithsonian Magazine*, April 2014, https://www.smithsonianmag.com/science-nature/does-thinking-fast-mean-youre-thinking-smarter-180950180/.

14. "Motivation in Adult Education Theory," Mighty Mustangs UTK, http://mightymustangsutk.weebly.com/motivation-in-adult-education-theory.html (Accessed March 14, 2018).

15. D. H. Schrunk, *Motivation in Education: Theory, Research, and Applications* (New York: Pearson Education, Inc., 2014), 237.

16. Daniel Pink, *Drive: The Surprising Truth About What Motivates Us* (New York: Riverhead Books, 2011), 10.

17. Ibid, 10.

18. Kenneth W. Thomas, *Intrinsic Motivation at Work: What Really Drives Employee Engagement* (Audiogo, 2012), 47.

19. Natasha Bowman, "Do This, Not That: 10 Ways You Accidentally Contribute to Employee Disengagement," *Forbes Community Voice* (blog),

Forbes.com, July 2017, https://www.forbes.com/sites/forbescoachescouncil/2017/07/13/do-this-not-that-10-ways-you-accidentally-contribute-to-employee-disengagement/#114d98132d9a.

20. Bob Moritz, "The US Chairman of PWC on Keeping Millennials Engaged," *Harvard Business Review*, November 2014, https://hbr.org/2014/11/the-us-chairman-of-pwc-on-keeping-millennials-engaged.

21. "Workforce Purpose Index," Imperative.com, https://cdn.imperative.com/media/public/Purpose_Index_2015 (Accessed March 14, 2018).

22. Philip H. Mervis, http://www.sesp.northwestern.edu/masters-learning-and-organizational-change/knowledge-lens/stories/2016/the-power-of-purpose-how-organizations-are-making-work-more-meaningful.html.

23. Carol Dweck, "The Power of Believing that You Can Improve," TEDx, November 2014, https://www.ted.com/talks/carol_dweck_the_power_of_believing_that_you_can_improve.

24. Carol Dweck, *Mindset* (New York: Ballantine Books, 2007).

25. Carol Dweck, "The Right Mindset for Success," *Harvard Business Review*, Education, https://hbr.org/2012/01/the-right-mindset-for-success (Accessed March 14, 2018).

26. Carol Dweck, "The Power of Believing that You Can Improve," TEDx, November 2014, https://www.ted.com/talks/carol_dweck_the_power_of_believing_that_you_can_improve.

27. Satya Nadella, interview by Dina Bass, Bloomberg.com August 2016, https://www.bloomberg.com/features/2016-satya-nadella-interview-issue/ (Accessed March 14, 2018).

28. Ibid.

29. Ibid.

30. Angela Lee Duckworth, "Grit: The Power of Passion and Perseverance," Ted Talks, April, 2013, Education, https://www.ted.com/talks/angela_lee_duckworth_grit_the_power_of_passion_and_perseverance#t-78738.

31. Aleszu Bajak, "Lectures Aren't Just Boring, They're Ineffective Too," *Science*, May 12, 2014, http://www.sciencemag.org/news/2014/05/lectures-arent-just-boring-theyre-ineffective-too-study-finds.

32. Audie Cornish and Sam Gringlas, "Vermont Medical School Says Goodbye to Lectures," NPR.org, August 3, 2017, https://www.npr.org/sections/health-shots/2017/08/03/541411275/vermont-medical-school-says-goodbye-to-lectures.

33. "What is Reflective Practice?" *Skills You Need*, https://www.skillsyouneed.com/ps/reflective-practice.html (Accessed March 14, 2018).

34. Dorothy Leonard, "How to Build Expertise in a New Field," *Harvard Business Review*, April 8, 2015, Developing Employees, https://hbr.org/2015/04/how-to-build-expertise-in-a-new-field#comment-section.

35. Ibid.

36. Tracy Maylett, "6 Ways to Encourage Autonomy with Your Employees," *Entrepreneur,* March 4, 2016, Leadership, https://www.entrepreneur.com/article/254030.

37. Guadalupe Gonzales, "How Elon Musk, Warren Buffet and Other Billionaires Learn New Things," Inc.com, September 20, 2017, https://www.inc.com/video/how-brilliant-billionaires-learn-new-things.html?cid=readmorevideoimage.

38. Drake Baer and Shana Lebowitz, "14 Books that Inspired Elon Musk," *Business Insider UK,* October 2015, http://uk.businessinsider.com/elon-musk-favorite-books-2015-10.

39. Richard Feloni, "14 Books Mark Zuckerberg Thinks Everyone Should Read," *Business Insider UK,* October 2015, http://www.businessinsider.com/mark-zuckerberg-book-recommendations-2015-10/#why-nations-fail-by-daren-acemolu-and-james-robinson-1.

40. Michael Simmons, "Bill Gates, Warren Buffet and Oprah Winfrey All Use the 5-Hour Rule," *Observer,* May 2016, http://observer.com/2016/08/bill-gates-warren-buffett-and-oprah-winfrey-all-use-the-5-hour-rule/.

41. Kai Sato, *Entrepreneur,* https://www.entrepreneur.com/article/233444.

Chapter 2

1. Jennifer Reingold, "What the Heck Is Angela Ahrendts Doing at Apple?" *Fortune,* September 10, 2015, http://fortune.com/2015/09/10/angela-ahrendts-apple/.

2. Ibid.

3. Ibid.

4. Ilan Brat, "Starbucks to Pay Full Cost of Online Degree for Employees," *Wall Street Journal,* April 6, 2015, Business, www.wsj.com/articles/starbucks-to-pay-full-cost-of-online-degree-for-employees-1428359401.

5. William Arruda, "5 Great Companies that Get Corporate Culture Right," *Forbes,* August 17, 2017, Leadership, www.forbes.com/sites/william arruda/2017/08/17/5-great-companies-that-get-corporate-culture-right/#4d5e82241582.

6. Larry Alton, "How Millennials Are Reshaping What's Important in Corporate Culture," *Forbes,* June 20, 2017, Under 30, www.forbes.com/sites/larryalton/2017/06/20/how-millennials-are-reshaping-whats-important-in-corporate-culture/#5e3062472dfb.

7. Deloitte, "Cultural Issues in Mergers and Acquisitions," (PDF), www2.deloitte.com/content/dam/Deloitte/us/Documents/mergers-acqisitions/us-ma-consulting-cultural-issues-in-ma-010710.pdf (Accessed March 14 2018).

8. Sarah Jacobs, Áine Cain, and Jacquelyn Smith, "A Look Inside $23 Billion LinkedIn's New York Office, Where Employees Enjoy Perks Like Free Gourmet Meals and a Speakeasy Hidden in the Empire State Building,"

Business Insider UK, November 4, 2016, Tech, http://uk.businessinsider.com/a-look-inside-linkedins-empire-state-building-office-2016-10.

9. Benjamin Snyder, "14% of Zappos' Staff Left After Being Offered Exit Pay," *Fortune*, May 18, 2015, Retail, http://fortune.com/2015/05/08/zappos-quit-employees/.

10. Reid Hoffman, MastersofScale.com, podcast, June 27, 2017, https://mastersofscale.com/.

11. Richard Feloni, "LinkedIn Founder Reid Hoffman Shares the Management Epiphany that Took His Company to the Next Level," *Business Insider UK*, March 2, 2016, Strategy, http://uk.businessinsider.com/reid-hoffman-explains-why-corporate-culture-needs-to-be-codified-2016-3.

12. Jodi Kantor and David Streitfeld, "Inside Amazon: Wrestling Big Ideas in a Bruising Workplace," *New York Times*, August 15, 2015, Business Day, www.nytimes.com/2015/08/16/technology/inside-amazon-wrestling-big-ideas-in-a-bruising-workplace.html?mcubz=0.

13. Davey Alba, "Ellen Pao Ends Her Lawsuit Against Kleiner Perkins," *Wired*, September 10, 2015, Business, www.wired.com/2015/09/ellen-pao-ends-lawsuit-kleiner-perkins/.

14. T. C. Sottek, "Former Engineer Says Uber is a Nightmare of Sexism," *The Verge*, February 19, 2017, www.theverge.com/2017/2/19/14664474/uber-sexism-allegations.

15. Ron Williams, "A Positive, High Performance Culture Can Reap the Biggest Rewards. Ignoring Culture Can Result in Disaster," LinkedIn, June 5, 2017, www.linkedin.com/pulse/positive-high-performance-culture-can-reap-biggest-rewards-williams/.

16. Josh Bersin, "Becoming Irresistible: a New Model for Employee Engagement," *Deloitte Review*, January 16, 2015, https://dupress.deloitte.com/dup-us-en/deloitte-review/issue-16/employee-engagement-strategies.html.

17. Melissa Llarena, "How Not to Lose Your New Employees in Their First 45 Days." *Forbes*, July 19, 2013, Online: https://www.forbes.com/sites/85broads/2013/07/19/how-not-to-lose-your-new-employees-in-their-first-45-days/#2aff06073be3.

18. B. Bhaswati, "Employee Onboarding at Facebook, Google and Apple," *Capabiliti*, February 24, 2016, https://blog.capabiliti.co/employee-onboarding-facebook-google-apple/.

19. Daniel Pink, *Drive, The Surprising Truth about What Motivates Us* (London: Canongate, 2011).

20. Ibid, 90.

21. Charles Arthur, "Yahoo Chief Bans Working from Home," *Guardian*, February 25, 2013, Technology, www.theguardian.com/technology/2013/feb/25/yahoo-chief-bans-working-home.

22. Reid Hoffman, *The Alliance: Managing Talent in the Networked Age* (Boston: Harvard Business Review Press, 2014).

23. "Growithus: professional development within Pirelli," YouTube, November 23, 2016, https://www.youtube.com/watch?v=3fEnYtZad3k.

24. Joanne Wells, "10 Ways to Build a Culture of Continuous Learning," Association for Talent Development, February 2017, www.td.org/Publi cations/Magazines/TD/TD-Archive/2017/02/Webex-10-Ways-to-Build-a -Culture-of-Continuous-Learning.

Chapter 3

1. Victoria Hoffman, "The Current State of Corporate Personalized Learning," *eLearning Industry*, May 30, 2017, https://elearningindustry.com/ corporate-personalized-learning-current-state.

2. Ibid.

3. Todd Rose (director of the Harvard Mind, Brain, and Education graduate program), interview by Kelly Palmer, April 2017.

4. Ibid.

5. Dale J. Stephens, *Hacking Your Education* (New York: Penguin Random House, 2013).

6. Dale J. Stephens (founder of social movement UnCollege), interview by Kelly Palmer, November 2017.

7. Laurie Pickard, *Don't Pay for Your MBA: The Faster, Cheaper, Better Way to Get the Education You Need* (Amacom, 2017).

8. Tim Walker, "As More Schools Look to Personalized Learning, Teaching May Be About to Change," *NeaToday*, June 9, 2017, http://neatoday .org/2017/06/09/personalized-learning/.

9. Todd Rose (director of the Harvard Mind, Brain, and Education graduate program), interview by Kelly Palmer, April 2017.

10. Timothy Scott, "Education Technology, Surveillance and America's Authoritarian Democracy," *Narrative Disruptions* (blog), https://narrative disruptions.wordpress.com/education-technology-surveillance-and -americas-authoritarian-democracy/ (Accessed March 14, 2018).

11. Todd Rose (director of the Harvard Mind, Brain, and Education graduate program), interview by Kelly Palmer, April 2017.

12. Ibid.

13. Rico Rodriguez (software developer), interview by Kelly Palmer, October 2017.

14. Todd Rose (director of the Harvard Mind, Brain, and Education graduate program), interview by Kelly Palmer, April 2017.

15. Guy Kawasaki, "How to Rock Social Media" Lynda.com, September 19, 2015, https://www.lynda.com/Facebook-tutorials/How-Rock-Social-Media/ 373993-2.html.

16. Brian Honigman, "Marketing Foundations: Social Media," Lynda.com, June 19, 2017, https://www.lynda.com/Marketing-tutorials/Marketing

-Foundations-Social-Media/567790-2.html?srchtrk=index%3a1%0alink
typeid%3a2%0aq%3aMarketing+Foundations%3a+Social+Media%0a
page%3a1%0as%3arelevance%0asa%3atrue%0aproducttypeid%3a2.

17. https://brilliant.org.

18. Todd Rose (director of the Harvard Mind, Brain, and Education graduate
    program), interview by Kelly Palmer, April 2017.

Chapter 4

1. "Exponential Growth of Data," *Inside Big Data*, February 16, 2017, https://
   insidebigdata.com/2017/02/16/the-exponential-growth-of-data/.

2. Research Report, "How the Workforce Learns in 2016," *Degreed*, https://get.
   degreed.com/how-the-workforce-learns-in-2016-report (Accessed March
   14, 2018).

3. Tim Quinlan presents at Degreed LENS, San Francisco, September 2016
   https://degreed.com/videos/degreed-lens-sf--tim-quinlan?d=3547967
   &view=false.

4. TheSecondCityWorks.com, http://secondcityworks.com/offerings/licensed
   -video/ (Accessed March 14, 2018).

5. John B. Horrigan, "Lifelong Learning and Technology," *Pew Research
   Center*, March 22, 2016, http://www.pewinternet.org/2016/03/22/lifelong
   -learning-and-technology/.

6. Sal Khan (founder, Khan Academy), interview by Kelly Palmer, February
   2018.

7. Khan Academy Annual Report, http://khanacademyannualreport.org/
   (Accessed March 14, 2018).

8. Clive Thompson, "How Khan Academy Is Changing the Rules of Education," *Wired*, July 15, 2011, https://www.wired.com/2011/07/ff_khan/.

9. "Passion vs. Paycheck? Bank of America, Khan Academy Help New Grads
   Succeed in Life's Next Chapter," *Bank of America*, June 7, 2017, http://
   newsroom.bankofamerica.com/press-releases/community-development/
   passion-vs-paycheck-bank-america-khan-academy-help-new-grads-su.

10. Ibid.

11. Stanford Undergraduate Admissions, Stanford.edu, https://admission
    .stanford.edu/apply/selection/profile16.html (Accessed March 14, 2018).

12. Tamar Lewin, "Instruction for Masses Knocks Down Campus Walls,"
    New York Times, March 4, 2012, Education, http://www.nytimes.com/
    2012/03/05/education/moocs-large-courses-open-to-all-topple-campus
    -walls.html.

13. Chen Zhenghao, Brandon Alcorn, Gayle Christensen, Nicholas Eriksson,
    Daphne Koller, and Ezekiel J. Emanuel, "Who's Benefiting from MOOCs,
    and Why," *Harvard Business* Review, September 22, 2015, Education,
    https://hbr.org/2015/09/whos-benefiting-from-moocs-and-why.

14. Ibid.

15. https://www.coursera.org/learn/gcp-big-data-ml-fundamentals.

16. "Coursera Partners with AXA to Bring World-Class Learning into the Workplace," BusinessWire.com, July 18, 2017, http://www.business wire.com/news/home/20170717006299/en/Coursera-Partners-AXA -Bring-World-Class-Learning-Workplace.

17. "Coursera Launches Coursera for Business, an Enterprise Platform for Workforce Development at Scale," Marketwired.com, August 31, 2016, http://www.marketwired.com/press-release/coursera-launches-coursera -business-enterprise-platform-workforce-development-scale-2154565.htm.

18. Monika Hamori, "Can MOOCs Solve Your Training Problem?" *Harvard Business Review*, January–February 2018, https://hbr.org/2018/01/ can-moocs-solve-your-training-problem.

19. Jenna Sargent, "Google and Pluralsight Partner on Developer Skills and Compuware and SonarSource's COBOL Code Coverage," *SD Times*, January 4, 2018, https://sdtimes.com/cobol/sd-times-news-digest-google-pluralsight-partner- developer-skills-compuware-sonarsources-cobol-code-coverage/.

20. Alex Khurgin, "How Microlearning Will Shape the Future of Work," *Association for Talent Development*, August 30, 2017, https://www.td.org/ insights/how-microlearning-will-shape-the-future-of-work.

21. https://www.grovo.com.

22. Maksim Ovsyannikov (former vice president of product, Grovo), interview by Kelly Palmer, February 2018.

23. Ibid.

24. Ibid.

25. James Densmore (director of data science, Degreed), interview by Kelly Palmer, July 2017.

26. Karie Willyerd (author, *Stretch: How to Future-Proof Yourself for Tomorrow's Workplace*), interview by Kelly Palmer, November 2017.

27. Ibid.

Chapter 5

1. Josh Bersin, "Watch Out, Corporate Learning: Here Comes Disruption," *Forbes*, March 28, 2017, www.forbes.com/sites/joshbersin/2017/03/28/watch -out-corporate-learning-here-comes-disruption/#5ebb9533dc59.

2. Art Kohn, "Brain Science: The Forgetting Curve—The Dirty Secret of Corporate Training," *Learning Solutions Magazine*, March 13, 2014, www.learning solutionsmag.com/articles/1379/brain-science-the-forgetting-curvethe -dirty-secret-of-corporate-training.

3. Jacob Morgan, "The Top 10 Factors for On-the-Job Employee Happiness," *Forbes*, December 15, 2014, www.forbes.com/sites/jacobmorgan/2014/12/15/ the-top-10-factors-for-on-the-job-employee-happiness/#328f1c5c5afa.

4. T. Cornelissen, et al. "Peer Effects in the Workplace," American Economic Review 107 no 2 (2017): 425–56.

5. Albert Bandura, *Social Learning Theory* (New York: General Learning Press, 1977).

6. Jaime Casap (education evangelist, Google), interview by Kelly Palmer, June 2017.

7. Jennifer Porter, "Why You Should Make Time for Self-Reflection (Even if You Hate Doing It)," *Harvard Business Review*, March 21, 2017, https://hbr.org/2017/03/why-you-should-make-time-for-self-reflection-even-if-you-hate-doing-it.

8. Peter Drucker, DruckerInstitute.com, February 16, 2011, http://www.druckerinstitute.com/2011/02/high-time-for-think-time/.

9. Cadie Thompson, "The Top 10 Skills that Will Be in Demand by All Employers by 2020," *Business Insider UK*, January 21, 2016, http://uk.businessinsider.com/wef-report-skills-workers-need-2016-1/?r=US&IR=T/#10-cognitive-flexibility-will-continue-to-be-an-important-skill-1.

10. Fred Kofman, *Conscious Business—How to Build Value through Value* (Colorado: Sounds True Inc., 2014).

11. Ibid.

12. Jaime Casap (education evangelist, Google), interview by Kelly Palmer, June 2017.

13. Ruth Helyer, "Learning through Reflection: The Critical Role of Reflection in Work-Based Learning (WBL)," *Journal of Work-Applied Management* 7, no 1: 15–27. Online at www.emeraldinsight.com/doi/full/10.1108/JWAM-10-2015-003.

14. Charles Duhigg, "What Google Learned from Its Quest to Build the Perfect Team," *New York Times*, February 25, 2016, www.nytimes.com/2016/02/28/magazine/what-google-learned-from-its-quest-to-build-the-perfect-team.html.

15. Ibid.

16. Michael Grothaus, "The Six Google Tech Talks Every Developer Should Watch," Fast Company.com, August 19, 2013, www.fastcompany.com/3015964/the-six-google-tech-talks-every-developer-should-watch.

17. "Leaders Teaching Leaders" Adobe Life, January 9, 2013, http://blogs.adobe.com/adobelife/2013/01/09/leaders-teaching-leaders/.

18. Ibid.

19. Ibid.

20. Shawn Achor, "The Benefits of Peer-to-Peer Praise at Work," *Harvard Business Review*, February 19, 2016, https://hbr.org/2016/02/the-benefits-of-peer-to-peer-praise-at-work.

21. Paula Newton, "Jack Welch Online MBA," Intelligent HQ, February 4, 2015, www.intelligenthq.com/business-education/inside-the-online-jack-welch-mba/.

22. Jeff Kauflin, "Jack Welch's Third Act: an Online MBA Program that's Thriving," *Forbes*, November 22, 2016, www.forbes.com/sites/jeffkauflin/2016/11/22/jack-welchs-third-act-an-online-mba-program-thats-thriving/2/#66b40d6f121c.

23. Brigitte Cutshall, "AltMBA Is Like a Tough Sailing Adventure," *The Blog, Huffington Post*, July 30, 2015, www.huffingtonpost.com/brigitte-cutshall/altmba-is-like-a-tough-sa_b_7904916.html.

24. Joanne Heyman (founder and CEO, Heyman Partners and adjunct professor, Columbia University), interview by Kelly Palmer, July 2017.

25. Ibid.

26. Wouter de Bres (founder, Bread & Pepper, and Gibbon), interview by Kelly Palmer, August 2017.

27. www.Dribbble.com.

28. Ibid.

29. Jennifer Porter, "Why You Should Make Time for Self-Reflection (Even if You Hate Doing It)," *Harvard Business Review*, March 21, 2017, https://hbr.org/2017/03/why-you-should-make-time-for-self-reflection-even-if-you-hate-doing-it.

30. Yael Bacharach, "How to Give Constructive Feedback," Inc. www.inc.com/yael-bacharach/how-to-give-feedback-developmental-conversations.html (Accessed on March 14, 2018).

31. Susan M. Heathfield, "Receive Feedback with Grace and Dignity," The Balance, October 17, 2016, www.thebalance.com/receive-feedback-with-grace-and-dignity-1916643.

Chapter 6

1. Bror Saxberg (vice president of learning science, Chan-Zuckerberg Initiative (CZI)), interview by Kelly Palmer, November 2017.

2. Nigel Paine (learning thought leader and author, *The Learning Challenge*), interview by Kelly Palmer, November 2017.

3. Steve Jobs, "Computers Are Like Bicycles for Our Minds," YouTube, June 1, 2006, https://www.youtube.com/watch?v=ob_GX50Za6c.

4. Nigel Paine (learning thought leader and author, *The Learning Challenge*), interview by Kelly Palmer, November 2017.

5. Anne Fulton (founder, Fuel50), interview by Kelly Palmer, January 2018.

6. Global Disruptive HR Technologies Report, IQPC, 2017, https://www.fuel50.com/2018/01/hr-tech-global-report.

7. Anne Fulton (founder, Fuel50), interview by Kelly Palmer, January 2018.

8. https://www.taprootfoundation.org/.

9. Imperative, "2015 Workforce Purpose Index," (PDF) https://cdn.imperative.com/media/public/Purpose_Index_2015.

10. Aaron Hurst, *The Purpose Economy: How Your Desire for Impact, Personal Growth and Community is Changing the World* (Boise: Elevate, 2014).
11. Aaron Hurst (founder, Taproot Foundation and Imperative), interview by Kelly Palmer, November, 2017.
12. Imperative, "Purpose in Higher Education," (PDF), https://cdn.imperative.com/media/public/Purpose_in_Higher_Education.pdf.
13. Imperative, "2015 Workforce Purpose Index," (PDF), https://cdn.imperative.com/media/public/Purpose_Index_2015.
14. Thomas L. Friedman, "How to Get a Job at Google," *New York Times*, February 22, 2014, Sunday Review, https://www.nytimes.com/2014/02/23/opinion/sunday/friedman-how-to-get-a-job-at-google.html.
15. Emily Foote (co-founder, Practice), interview by Kelly Palmer, December 19, 2017.
16. Ibid.
17. Sam Herring (founder, Intrepid Learning), interview by Kelly Palmer, December 15, 2017.
18. "Microsoft Transforms Global Salesforce with Revolutionary Corporate MOOC," (PDF), Intrepidlearning.com, https://www.intrepidlearning.com/wp-content/uploads/2016/11/Intrepid-CaseStudy_MSFT_BusinessSchool.pdf.
19. Ibid.
20. Sam Herring (founder, Intrepid Learning), interview by Kelly Palmer, December 15, 2017.
21. Innovator's Guide to Learning Technology, Degreed 2017.

Chapter 7

1. Peter M. Senge, *The Fifth Discipline: The Art and Practice of the Learning Organization* (New York: Doubleday, 1990), cited in book jacket.
2. Susie Lee (head of global business solutions, Degreed), interview by Kelly Palmer, February 2018.
3. Ibid.
4. Ibid.
5. Louis Columbus, "LinkedIn's Fastest Growing Jobs Today Are in Data Science and Machine Learning," Forbes, December 11, 2017, Tech, https://www.forbes.com/sites/louiscolumbus/2017/12/11/linkedins-fastest-growing-jobs-today-are-in-data-science-machine-learning/#1db7c54751bd.
6. Deanna Mulligan, "We Have the Tools to Reskill for the Future. Where is the Will to Use Them?" World Economic Forum, January 19, 2018, https://www.weforum.org/agenda/2018/01/tools-reskill-future-will-labour-disruption-automation/.
7. Ibid.

8. Maksim Ovsyannikov (vice president of product at Degreed), interview by Kelly Palmer, March 2018.

9. "LinkedIn Workforce Report San Francisco Bay Area", January 5, 2018 https://www.linkedin.com/jobs/blog/linkedin-workforce-report-january-2018-san-francisco-ca.

10. Janice Burns (chief learning officer, MasterCard), from Degreed Client Impact Study, August 2017.

11. Towards Maturity, 2018, https://towardsmaturity.org/

12. Degreed webinar with Tony Gagliardo, August 15, 2017, http://webcasts.td.org/webinar/2256

13. Shum Attygalle, "Measuring What Matters," Axonify, The Knowledge Blog (webinar), June 23, 2017, https://axonify.com/blog/measuring-what-matters/.

14. Kristi Hedges, "How to Tell a Good Story," Forbes, December 11, 2013, https://www.forbes.com/sites/work-in-progress/2013/12/11/how-to-tell-a-good-story/#52c267eb584c.

Chapter 8

1. Thomas L. Friedman, *Thank You for Being Late: An Optimist's Guide to Thriving in the Age of Accelerations*, Kindle edition (New York: Farrar, Straus and Giroux, 2016), 31.

2. Ibid, 206.

3. Reid Wilson, "More Americans Have College Degrees than Ever Before," *The Hill*, March 4, 2017, http://thehill.com/homenews/state-watch/326995-census-more-americans-have-college-degrees-than-ever-before.

4. Steven Forth, "Skill and Expertise Management 2018. Preliminary Survey Results," Team Fit, January 29, 2018, http://hq.teamfit.co/skill-and-expertise-management-2018-preliminary-survey-results/.

5. http://www.skillsfuture.sg/AboutSkillsFuture.

6. "Bill McDermott: Never Too Old—or Young—to Learn and Grow," IESE Insight, March 20, 2018, http://www.ieseinsight.com/fichaMaterial.aspx?pk=148438&idi=2&origen=1&ar=15&buscador=1&general=learn&_ga=2.120077962.323679558.1530119839-1104372969.1530119839.

7. "Boeing announces details of $100 million employee education investment," Boeing, June 4, 2018, http://boeing.mediaroom.com/2018-06-04-Boeing-announces-details-of-100-million-employee-education-investment

8. Ibid.

9. Steven Pearlstein, "Marlin Steel's smart matrix for job and wage growth," *Washington Post*, December 12, 2014, https://www.washingtonpost.com/business/marlin-steels-smart-matrix-for-job-and-wage-growth/2014/12/12/977cd030-8151-11e4-81fd-8c4814dfa9d7_story.html?noredirect=on&utm_term=.c2b8569e0b54.

10. Ibid

11. Mikel Blake (web developer), interview by Kelly Palmer, February 2018.

12. http://www.mothercoders.org/.

13. Sal Khan (founder, Khan Academy), interview by Kelly Palmer, February 2018.

14. Jamie Merisotis, "Powerful New Technology Isn't Just Displacing Workers. It's Uncovering Learning Pathways to Employment in New Fields," Lumina Foundation, December 7, 2017, News &Views, https://www.luminafounda tion.org/news-and-views/powerful new-technology-isnt-just-displacing -workers-its-uncovering-learning-pathways-to-employment-in-new-fields.

Conclusion

1. Alan Walton (data scientist, Degreed), interview by Kelly Palmer, February 2018.

2. Tom Simonite, "Google's New Service Translates Languages Almost As Well As Humans Can," *MIT Technology Review*, September 27, 2016, https://www.technologyreview.com/s/602480/googles-new-service -translates-languages-almost-as-well-as-humans-can/.

3. "About Us," Deep Instinct, 2018, https://www.deepinstinct.com/who-we -are/#block1.

4. Christopher Moyer, "How Google's AlphaGo Beat a Go World Champion," *The Atlantic*, March 28, 2016, Technology, https://www.theatlantic.com/ technology/archive/2016/03/the-invisible-opponent/475611/.

5. Ian Sample, "'It's Able to Create Knowledge Itself': Google Unveils AI that Learns on Its Own," *Guardian*, October 18, 2017, Science, https://www .theguardian.com/science/2017/oct/18/its-able-to-create-knowledge-itself -google-unveils-ai-learns-all-on-its-own.

6. Daniel Susskind, *The Future of the Professions: How Technology Will Transform the Work of Human Experts* (Oxford: Oxford University Press, 2015).

7. Daniel Susskind, "3 Myths About the Future of Work (and Why They're Not True)," filmed December 2017 in Darmstadt, Germany, TED video, 15:48, https://www.ted.com/talks/daniel_susskind_3_myths_about_the _future_of_work_and_why_they_re_not_true#t-478070.

8. Ibid.

9. Garry Kasparov, "Don't Fear Intelligent Machines. Work With Them," Tiny TED, https://en.tiny.ted.com/talks/garry_kasparov_don_t_fear_intelligent _machines_work_with_them.

10. Ibid.

11. "Chapter 1: The Future of Jobs and Skills," The Future of Jobs Report, World Economic Forum, 2016, http://reports.weforum.org/future-of-jobs-2016/ chapter-1-the-future-of-jobs-and-skills/.

12. Lynda Gratton and Andrew Scott, *The 100-Year Life: Living and Working in an Age of Longevity* (London: Bloomsbury Information Ltd, 2016), 137.

13. Gratton and Scott, *The 100-Year Life*, 139.
14. Sal Khan (founder Khan Academy), interview by Kelly Palmer, February 2018.
15. Lynda Gratton and Andrew Scott, The *100-Year Life: Living and Working in an Age of Longevity* (London: Bloomsbury Information Ltd, 2016), 93.
16. Karie Willyerd (author, *The 2020 Workplace: How Innovative Companies Attract, Develop, and Keep Tomorrow's Employees Today*), interview by Kelly Palmer, November 2017.
17. Ibid.
18. Ibid.
19. Karie Willyerd, *Stretch: How to Future-Proof Yourself for Tomorrow's Workplace* (New Jersey: John Wiley, 2016).
20. Karie Willyerd (author, *The 2020 Workplace: How Innovative Companies Attract, Develop, and Keep Tomorrow's Employees Today*), interview by Kelly Palmer, November 2017.
21. Nigel Paine (author, *The Learning Challenge*), interview by Kelly Palmer, November 2017.
22. Delia Lloyd, "21st Century Skills for Older Workers," *The Oxford Institute of Population Ageing* (blog), University of Oxford, March 14, 2018, https://www.ageing.ox.ac.uk/blog/skills-for-older-workers?platform=hootsuite.
23. Christopher S. Rugaber, "Pay Gap Between College Grads and Everyone Else at a Record," *USA Today*, January 12, 2017, https://www.usatoday.com/story/money/2017/01/12/pay-gap-between-college-grads-and-everyone-else-record/96493348/.
24. Jaime Casap (education evangelist, Google), interview by Kelly Palmer, June 2017.
25. Ryan Craig and Brian Weed, "Helping New Grads Launch in the Workforce—And Why It's Vital to Companies," *Forbes*, January 19, 2018, Education, https://www.forbes.com/sites/ryancraig/2018/01/19/helping-new-grads-launch-in-the-workforce-and-why-its-vital-to-companies/#3f41fa1f2d8a.
26. Lydia Dishman, "These Are the Biggest Skills that New Graduates Lack," *FastCompany*, May 17, 2016, https://www.fastcompany.com/3059940/these-are-the-biggest-skills-that-new-graduates-lack.
27. Clayton M. Christensen, *The Innovator's Dilemma: When New Technologies Cause Great Firms to Fail* (Boston: Harvard Business Review Press, 2013).
28. Clayton Christensen (professor, Harvard Business School, and author, *The Innovator's Dilemma*), interview by Kelly Palmer, February 2018.
29. Whitney Johnson, *Build an A-Team: Play to Their Strengths and Lead Them Up the Learning Curve* (Boston: Harvard Business Review Press, 2018).
30. Whitney Johnson (author, *Build an A-Team: Play to Their Strengths and Lead Them Up the Learning Curve*), interview by Kelly Palmer, January 2018.
31. Ibid.
32. Karie Willyerd (author, *The 2020 Workplace: How Innovative Companies*

Attract, Develop, and Keep Tomorrow's Employees Today), interview by Kelly Palmer, November 2017.

33. "Millennial Careers: 2020 Vision," Manpower Group, https://www.man powergroup.com/wps/wcm/connect/660ebf65-144c-489e-975c-9f838294 c237/MillennialsPaper1_2020Vision_lo.pdf?MOD=AJPERES.

34. Sal Khan (founder, Khan Academy), interview by Kelly Palmer, February 2018.

35. Whitney Johnson, *Disrupt Yourself: Putting the Power of Disruptive Innovation to Work* (Abingdon: Routledge, 2015).

36. Whitney Johnson (author, *Build an A-Team: Play to Their Strengths and Lead Them Up the Learning Curve*), interview by Kelly Palmer, January 2018.

INDEX

A
accountability, 40
active learning, 16
Adobe, 95; "Leaders Teaching
    Leaders" program, 95
adult learning, 1, 7
Ahrendts, Angela, 23–24
Airbnb, xix, 18, 24, 33, 100, 176
AlphaGo system, 172
AlphaGo Zero, 172
Alter, Adam, 6–7
altMBA, 97
Apple, 23–25, 27, 30, 38, 108, 174
Arruda, William, 26
artificial intelligence, 2, 64, 70, 73,
    161, 172, 175, 184
AXA, 69

B
Bank of America, xviii, 34,
    43, 67, 134
Bartz, Carol, 28
Bezos, Jeff, 64
Blake, David, 31, 34, 65, 76, 115–118,
    132, 148, 152–153
Blake, Mikel, 152–154
Bock, Laszlo, 118
Boeing, 151, 154
Brin, Sergey, 64
Brown, Brené, 64
*Build an A-Team: Play to Their
    Strengths and Lead Them Up*

the Learning Curve (Whitney
    Johnson), 185
Burns, Janice, 133, 140–141, 145

C
Capozzi, Heidi, 151
career exploration, 56, 109–111
career paths, standard, 47–48
career pathways, 109–111
Casap, Jaime, 86, 93, 181
Chan, Priscilla, 2
Chan-Zuckerberg Initiative (CZI), 2
Chevron, 71
Christensen, Clayton, 183
"cloud mini-MBA" program, 126
Coca-Cola, 97
cognition, 3
collaboration, 38–40
company culture, 26; bad, 31;
    designing, 28–29; "kick butt
    and have fun," 27–28; LinkedIn,
    29–30; Netflix, 30; technology
    and, 127
company's labor market, 156–157
compensation, 9
competitive advantage, 12–13, xxi
compliance training, culture of,
    32–33
consumerization of content, 63–65
content overload, combating, xxii;
    consumerization of content,
    63–65; curating content,

72–75; digital learning strategy, 75–78; flipped classroom, 66–67; learning content libraries, 70; machine learning, 73–75; Massive Open Online Courses (MOOCs), 67–69; microlearning, 70–72; by overwhelmed learners, 78–81

continuous learning, culture of, 32, 34–36; developing, 42–44

contract assignment, skills quotient and, 166

control manager, 36, 38, 43

Cook, Tim, 23–24

corporate learning, 133–135

Coursera, 35, 68–69

Creative Live, 70

critical thinking skills, 11, 88; how to enhance, 102

culture, and learning, 25–27; guiding principle, 29–31; "kick butt and have fun," 27–28; types of learning cultures, 32–34

curating content, 72–75, 78–80

Curry, Steph, 188

Cutshall, Brigitte, 97–98

D

de Bres, Wouter, 99–100

DeepBlue, 173

deep learning, 171–172

DeepMind, 172–173

Degreed, 31, 34, 40, 43, 56, 60, 63, 74, 78, 115, 118, 132, 151; continuous learning culture at, 34–36; core principles of, 34–35

degree programs, skills quotient and, 169

Densmore, James, 74

developmental engagement, 10

Dev Mountain, 153

digital learning content, 64, 78

digital learning strategy, 75–78;

content for, 77; definition of, 76; impact of, 77–78; rationale for, 76–77

digital transformation, 24

Disrupt Yourself: Putting the Power of Disruptive Innovation to Work (Johnson), 188

Dominos, 122

Don't Pay for Your MBA: The Faster, Cheaper, Better Way to Get the Business Education You Need (Laurie Pickard), 50

Drive: The Surprising Truth about What Motivates Us (Daniel H. Pink), 7, 37

Dweck, Carol, 10–12

E

Eagleman, David, 4–5

eBay, 29, 55–57

Edx, 35, 68

e-learning, 63, 123

employee learning, 20–22

employee skills, 115–118

The End of Average: How We Succeed in a World that Values Sameness (Todd Rose), 6

Ericsson, 89

experiential learning, 111

expert revolution, xx–xxiii; hiring practices and, 154–156; relevant skills for company, 149–152; reskilling, 152–154; skills for nation, 149

F

Facebook, 8, 30, 33, 38, 54, 74, 100, 171–172

feedback, 17–18; giving constructive, 102–104; in peer-to-peer learning, 88–90

Flipboard, 100

flipped classroom, 66–67

Foote, Emily, 118–119, 121
Friedman, Thomas L., 148
Fuel50, 56, 108–111
FuelFactors, 111
fueling passion, idea of, 109–110
Fulton, Anne, 109–110
*The Future of the Professions: How
    Technology Will Transform the
    Work of Human Experts* (Daniel
    Susskind), 173

G
Gagliardo, Tony, 143
Gap, 71
Gates, Bill, 21, 64
Gates Foundation, 51, 66
General Electric (GE), 24–25, 184
Generation Z, 114
Gibbon, 99–100
Godin, Seth, 97
Goldman Sachs, 24
Google, 8, 25, 30, 38, 52–53, 61–62,
    66, 68, 74, 76, 78, 86, 93–95, 97,
    100, 137, 155, 172–173
Google/Pluralsight partnership, 70
Gratton, Lynda, 179
Greenblatt, Drew, 151–152
grit, 13
Grovo, 71

H
Hallmark, 97
hard skills, 123
Hastings, Reed, 30
Hedges, Kristi, 146
Helyer, Ruth, 93
Herring, Sam, 123–124
Heyman, Joanne, 97–98
high-impact learning organizations
    (HILOs), 25
hiring practices, 154–156, 184–185;
    skills quotient and, 165–166
Hoffer, Eric, 189

Hoffman, Reid, 30, 40–41
Hurst, Aaron, 9–10, 111–113

I
IBM, 74
Imperative (company), 9–10
individual learning, 62–63
Industrial Revolution, 46
The Innovator's Dilemma (Clayton
    Christensen), 183
INSEAD, 126
Intrepid, 125
*Intrinsic Motivation at Work:
    What Really Drives Employee
    Engagement* (Kenneth Thomas), 8
intrinsic motivators, 8
iSyndicate, 112

J
Jack Welch Management Institute
    (JWMI), 96
Jeffries, William, 16
JetBlue, 95–96
Jobs, Steve, 64, 108–109
jobs and careers, trend, 174–175
job seeking, skills quotient and, 165
Johnson, Dani, 145
Johnson, Whitney, 185

K
Kalanick, Travis, 31
Kasparov, Garry, 64, 173–174
Kawasaki, Guy, 55
Khan, Sal, 65, 158–159, 175
Khan Academy, 34, 65–67, 159,
    175–176, 187
Khim, Sue, 57
KIPP charter schools, 119
know-it-all employees, 20
knowledge: distinction between
    skills, 14; transfer, 14
knowledge-building, 15
Knowles, Malcolm, 7

L
labor market, proxies for skills in, 155–156; GPA/SAT/ACT score, 156; interviewing skills, 156; job titles, 155; logos on resumés, 155; pedigree of university, 155; references, 156
learners inherit the earth, 189
learning: adult, 7; for competitive advantage, 12–13, xxi; content, xxii; drivers for, 9–11; employee, xxii–xxiii; fast and being smart, 6–7; motivation, 3; neuromyths about, 4–5; from peers, xxii. *See also* peer-to-peer learning; personalized, xxi–xxii. *See also* personalized learning; power of, 24–25; science of, 2–4; steps to help employee, 20–22; truth about, 5–6; using right technology, xxii. *See also* technology for learning; vulnerability in, 19
learning agility, 54–57
learning analytics model (LAM), 136; at company level, 137, 140–141; at individual level, 137–138, 143–145; at industry level, 136–140; at organizational/team level, 137, 141–143
The Learning Challenge (Nigel Paine), 108, 178
learning content libraries, 70
learning credentials, 158–159
learning culture, 33; employer/ employee relationship, 40–42; illusion of control, 38–40; managers' influence on, 36–37
learning engineers, 2
Learning Loop, 16–18, 20; in peer-to-peer learning, 86–87
learning profile, 188–189
learning story, 146

learn-it-all employees, 20
lectures, 14
Lee, Susie, 134–136
Leonard, Dorothy, 21
Lguide, 123–124
lifelong learners, 1, 12, 59, 64
LinkedIn, 8, 29, 38, 77, 116, 126; peer-to-peer learning at, 90–92
LMS technologies, 124
Lumina Foundation, 161–163
Lynda.com, 55, 70, 144

M
machine-curated content, 79–80
machine learning, 73–75
Massive Open Online Courses (MOOCs), 50, 64, 67–70, 124, 127
MasterCard, 73, 111, 133–134, 140, 145
MasterClass.com, 188
Maylett, Tracy, 21
McDermott, Bill, 150
McNealy, Scott, 27
meaning, as driver for learning, 9–11
mentoring: mentors and role models, 188; skills quotient and, 167–168
Mercedes-Benz, 68–69
Meyer, Marissa, 39
microlearning, 70–72
Microsoft, 29, 97, 125–127
Mills, Jo, 109
mindset, 12–13, 20
Mindset: The New Psychology of Success (Carol Dweck), 10
Mirren, Helen, 188
Mirvis, Philip H., 10
moment of need, 62–63
Moodlerooms, 52
MotherCoders, 153
motivation, 3; extrinsic, 7; intrinsic, 7
Munden, Tim, xix
Musk, Elon, 21, 64

N
Nadella, Satya, 12, 28
NASA: Deep Space Network, 143; Jet
    Propulsion Laboratory (JPL), 143
necessary training, culture of, 32–33
Netflix, 25, 30, 45, 74
Nike, 97
No-Pay MBA, 50

O
Okamoto, Karl, 118–121
online learning resources, 63
OpenSesame, 70
Oracle, xv, 28, 38
overwhelmed learners, combating
    content overload by, 78–81;
    career and planning approach,
    81; curating of content, 78–80;
    recommended content, 80;
    setting learning goals, 81
Ovsyannikov, Maksim, 71–72

P
Palmer, Kelly, 17, 27–29, 37–38, 41,
    48–49, 53, 63, 76–77, 80, 83–84,
    90–92, 131, 142–143, 145, 176
Paine, Nigel, 108–109, 178–179
Pearlstein, Steven, 152
peer-to-peer learning, xxii, 83–84;
    building safe environment for,
    92–95, 104–105; generational
    differences and, 85–86; key
    skills for, 87–90, 100; learning
    experience, 99–100; at LinkedIn,
    90–92; MBA and, 96–98; peers
    as learning facilitators, 84–85;
    peer-to-peer recognition
    program, 95–96; process, 86–87
PepsiCo, 71
Perkins, Kleiner, 31
perseverance, 13
personalized learning, xxi–xxii; in
    action, 51–54; "average-based"

approaches, 47; at Brilliant.
    org, 57–58; developing skills,
    49–51; in education, 49–51;
    embracing, 59–60; standardized
    learning approach, 46;
    technology for, 59; through
    experience, 48–49
Pickard, Laurie, 50
Pink, Daniel H., 7–8, 37
Pluralsight, 70
power manager, 36
Practice (company), 121–122
practice of skills, 16–17
promotion, skills quotient and, 167
public relations program, 182
purpose orientation in learning, 9–11,
    111–114
purpose-oriented workers, 10,
    113–114
Python programming language,
    52–54

Q
Quinlan, Tim, 62–63, 134

R
recruiting, 154–156; internal, 166;
    skills quotient and, 165–166
reflection/reflecting, 18–19
resilience, 13
reskilling, 152–154; skills quotient
    and, 167
Rodriguez, Rico, 52
Rogers, Cameron, 54–55
Rose, Todd, 6–7, 47–51, 54, 59

S
Safari, 70
SAP, 38, 150
Saxberg, Bror, 2–3, 107
Schmidt, Eric, 28
Scott, Andrew, 175–176
Seamons, Ryan, 35

Sedol, Lee, 172
self-reflection skills, 87–88, 123; how
    to self-reflect, 100–102
Senge, Peter, 133
Silver, David, 172
skills: baby boomer generation
    and, 177–179; for collective
    intelligence and ability, 159–160;
    as currency, 157–158; for future,
    175–176; gap, closing, xx–xxi,
    20–21, 47, 70, 73, 132, 137, 140,
    149, 179–180; gig economy and,
    176–177; measuring, 161–162;
    for nation, 149; relevant for
    company, 149–152
skills development, xvii–xix, 56;
    companies, role in development
    of, 183–186; individuals, role
    in development of, 186–189;
    universities, role in development
    of, 180–183
SkillsFuture program, 149
skills inventory, skills quotient and,
    168
Skillsoft, 70
Skills Quotient (SQ), xxiii, 162–165;
    application of, 165–169
Skoll Foundation, 66
smiley sheets, 131
social curation, 79
Southwest Airlines, 25
S&P 500 companies, xv
Spotify, 74
Square, 100
standard career path, 47–48
Stephens, Dale, 49
Stephenson, Randall, xvii
*Stretch: How to Future-Proof
    Yourself for Tomorrow's
    Workplace* (Karie Willyerd), 75,
    178
Sun Microsystems, xv, 27–28
Susskind, Daniel, 173

T
"takeaways," 18–19
Taproot Foundation, 9, 112
Taylor, Fredrick, 46
Teach for America, 119
TeamFit, 148
team work, 123–127
technology for learning, 107–108;
    company culture and, 127;
    for creating learning
    "ecosystem," 128–130;
    Fuel50, 109–111; Lguide, 123;
    LMS technologies, 124; Massive
    Open Online Courses (MOOCs),
    127; VitalSource Technologies,
    125
TED (Technology, Education, and
    Design), 64, 77, 147
Telus International, 161–162
Tesla, 24
*Thank You for Being Late:
    An Optimist's Guide to
    Thriving in the Age of
    Accelerations* (Thomas L.
    Friedman), 148
*The Purpose Economy: How Your
    Desire for Impact, Personal
    Growth and Community Is
    Changing the World* (Hurst),
    113–114
Thomas, Kenneth, 8
training, 14–15; skills quotient and,
    168–169
Treehouse, 70
Twitter, 54, 99–100

U
Udacity, 68–69
Udemy, 70
UnCollege, 49–50
Unilever, 43
universities, role in development of
    skills, 180–183

V
VitalSource Technologies, 125
vulnerability in learning, 19

W
Walton, Alan, 171, 174
Welch, Jack, 96–97
Whole Foods, 97
Williams, Ron, 31
Willyerd, Karie, 75, 81, 177–178, 186
Workforce Purpose Index, 114
workforce transitions, xvi–xvii
*The 2020 Workplace: How Innovative
    Companies Attract, Develop,
    and Keep Tomorrow's Employees
    Today* (Karie Willyerd), 177

workplace cultures, 27
wrong data, effect of, 145

Y
Yahoo!, 17, 29, 38–39, 100, 144
*The 100-Year Life: Living and
    Working in an Age of Longevity*
    (Andrew Scott),
    175–176
YouTube, 64–65, 77

Z
Zappos, 25, 30
ZenDesk, 100
Zinch, 116–117
Zuckerberg, Mark, 2, 22